Heaven's Ache

ALLYCE FOGLE-LOGUE

Heaven's Ache

A Walk Through the Psalms with Lament and Hope

invite
PRESS

Plano, Texas

Heaven's Ache
A Walk Through the Psalms with Lament and Hope
Copyright 2025 by Allyce Fogle-Logue.

All rights reserved.

This book is printed on acid-free, elemental chlorine-free paper.

ISBN: Paperback 978-1-963265-66-8; eBook 978-1-963265-67-5

All scripture quotations, unless otherwise indicated, are taken from the Holy Bible, New Living Translation (NLT), copyright © 1996. Used by permission of Tyndale House Publishers, Inc., Wheaton, Illinois 60189. All rights reserved.

Scripture quotations marked NIV are taken from the Holy Bible, New International Version®, NIV®. Copyright © 1973, 1978, 1984, 2011 by Biblica, Inc.™ Used by permission of Zondervan. All rights reserved worldwide.

Scripture quotations marked ESV are from The Holy Bible, English Standard Version® (ESV), copyright © 2001 by Crossway Bibles, a publishing ministry of Good News Publishers. Used by permission. All rights reserved.

Scripture quotations marked KJV are from the King James or Authorized Version of the Bible, which is in the public domain.

Scripture quotations marked GNT are from the Good News Translation® in Today's English Version, Second Edition, Copyright © 1992 by American Bible Society. Used by permission. All rights reserved.

Scripture quotations marked NCV are from The Holy Bible, New Century Version®. Copyright © 2005 by Thomas Nelson, Inc. Used by permission. All rights reserved.

Scripture quotations marked TLB are from The Living Bible copyright © 1971 by Tyndale House Foundation. Used by permission of Tyndale House Publishers Inc., Carol Stream, Illinois 60188. All rights reserved.

25 26 27 28 29 30 31 32 33 34—10 9 8 7 6 5 4 3 2 1
MANUFACTURED in the UNITED STATES of AMERICA

Acknowledgements

To those who hurt to depths they didn't know possible, this book is for you. May its contents spark healing and hope in a God who works in even the most desperate circumstances. Lament like you mean it.

In memory of Sara Carolyn Dicken, the first writer of my family.

It takes a special person to be married to a pastor and writer. David Logue is that person for me. David, you are my greatest earthly gift and better than my best imaginations.

Paul and Heidi Fogle are the two most supportive parents a daughter could have. You are my champions and advocates. To my in-laws, Jesse and Ann Logue—how fortunate I am to have joined this family with your thoughtfulness and intentionality. To my siblings, both biological (Ben) and gained through marriage (Erin, Rachel, Aaron, Andy, and Brittany), I'm thankful for each of your unique, wise influences on my life. To the two boys who made me an aunt, you have changed my heart, and I cannot wait to see you step into all that God has for you. To my church, college, and seminary community, this book has your fingerprints all over it because of the way you love like Jesus.

Len Wilson and the team at Invite Ministries, you took a risk on a new(ish) author. Thank you for trusting in this vision with me.

Thanks to two exemplary pastors, Rev. Richard Morris and Rev. Dr. Cory Hartman. Both men are beloved teachers and mentors, who show in daily life that the Kingdom of Heaven is for real. Cory and Kelly—your prayer and encouragement throughout this book (and in life) has served as water in the droughts.

Introduction

Who writes a book about lament? Well, that would be me.

I am not a particularly sad person. But sadness *is* one of the easiest emotions for me to access. As a pastor, I encounter sadness on a regular basis, and I've noticed a trend in all of my ministry contexts. Many people experiencing grief, sadness, and pain would prefer to distract themselves from their hurt as opposed to processing through complex emotions.

Who needs to think about why we are hurting when we have Netflix to numb our minds? Amazon at the punch of a button to bring us something that gives us a solid five-minute dopamine hit? Alcohol to forget about life? Sex to erase feelings?

For the longest time, I didn't understand—why the denial? And then I encountered a loss in my own life, and suddenly, I got it. The temptation to numb myself to the world around me was overwhelming for a time, but friends and family encouraged me to ask hard questions about my faith and practice what I (figuratively and literally) preached.

The Psalms became a haven for me to study and process grief and loss. An Old Testament professor of mine used to say that the Psalms are a diary of the range of human emotion. As it turns out, there are a significant number of Psalms created for the purpose of lament.

Lament was a normal, prevalent practice in the Bible. In times of grief, a period of mourning was instituted. Clothing was torn, hair was ripped out, and people would hire individuals to collectively mourn over losses. Those living in antiquity took their lamenting seriously.

In a seminary service, I once heard Julie Tennent give a thoughtful definition of lament as an active, faithful, and biblical response to the grief, pain, struggle, and suffering that we have as part of our humanity. Tennent suggests that when we partake in lament actively, faithfully, and biblically, we can honor God.[1]

Lament as an Active Response

When we actively lament, we do not passively set aside our grief, overlook it, or pretend it isn't there. We don't distract ourselves with work, online shopping, sex, food, or other things that numb us. Lamenting vocalizes our hearts. We grieve the hurt, the loss, and the stress that we are individually and collectively experiencing. God's shoulders are broad enough to handle our pain. Active response to lament is turning towards, not away, from God. Lament is to be in God's presence—to trust that He hears our pleas and ultimately promises to deliver us from the hurt we experience in this world.

Lament as a Faithful Response

To faithfully lament is to acknowledge our feelings but trust them less than God, His character, and His promises. Lament happens individually but also corporately. Corporate lament engages our community, providing support of encouragement in light of God's faithfulness.

Lament as a Biblical Response

At the initiation of the earth and the fall of humanity, God preceded us in lament. Therefore, when we lament, we may mirror God's original lament.

Tennent notes that in Genesis 3:9 (NIV), God asks questions of lament when engaging with Adam. When He asks, "Where are you?", God is lamenting a broken relationship. God asks, "Who told you that you were naked?" and "Have you eaten from the tree that I commanded you not to eat from?" (3:11 NIV). In these circumstances, God laments evil and brokenness in the world. Finally, God asks, "How could you have done such a thing?" (Genesis 3:13 NCV). Here, God laments betrayal and broken loyalty.[2]

Interestingly, when God laments of the world, He remembers to look ahead. He remembers grace, mercy, and love. He remembers that one day, nothing will be able to separate us from His love, despite the loss He has experienced in Genesis in His broken relationship with humanity.

We worship a triune God, and if God the Father laments in Genesis, we recognize that so did the Son and Holy Spirit.

Jesus enters lament with us before and while dying on the cross. In Matthew 26:38, Jesus tells his disciples in the Garden of Gethsemane that his "soul is crushed with grief to the point of death." In Matthew 27, we see Jesus being nailed on the cross, mocked, and humiliated. At his death, he was forsaken by God, and the weight of all sin rested upon him. Jesus understands lament and brokenness; Jesus knew what the end of his life would look like. Yet, throughout his ministry, Jesus makes repeated references to the time of his resurrection. His eyes are looking ahead at the big picture.

The Holy Spirit acts in lament and advocates on our behalf while we lament. The Holy Spirit groans with us in our lament and bears witness to the resurrection by continuing Christ's work, working in each of us so that we might transform the world and so that we might live into the resurrection, hope, and promises that God has made us to light our path and secure our way to eternity.

Active, faithful, and biblical lament acknowledges the loss, grief, and uncertainty that we may feel yet continues to look forward to hope in what the resurrection has set in motion and will accomplish: the restoration of humanity through a new heaven and a new earth.

Until that time of full restoration, I have come to recognize that hardship and suffering comes to each person in some form. To be human is to encounter suffering. To avoid suffering is to avoid living by numbing ourselves to reality. If suffering is a part of the human life, shouldn't we understand how to walk through hardship in a God-honoring way? In my estimate, learning to lament is fundamental to growing in faithfulness to God as we seek to be redeemed creations.

I developed this resource for anyone who may be in the midst of suffering and desires to process their circumstances before God in such a way that promotes healing and wholeness. I also wrote this book to help the church recover lament as a tool and discipline to prepare spiritually for when hardship comes.

It is my hope that in the contents of these pages, you may find, identify with, and process through these Psalms of lament. The Psalms explored in this text showcase both individual and communal forms of lament. You may choose to read through this book alone or with a group. Each day, you will be given a Psalm to read, and you will be invited to explore what that Psalm means, implies, and how we might respond to God's Word. For further reflection, you will receive questions to consider as part of your devotional time.

Here is the hope that lament offers: it is meant to be seasonal. When we invite God's presence to heal us and cooperate with the Spirit's promptings, we may heal. When a season of lament ends, joy comes and with it, healing, wholeness, and restoration. I know this because I have experienced it. *I* can't heal you. I'm not convinced that *we* can heal ourselves. But I know *someOne* who can. The God of all the ages, who loves His children, sees and recognizes a groaning creation, and if we would be willing, He would draw Himself to us and make us new.

Day One: Psalm 3

What Does This Mean?

The opening to this Psalm suggests that David has enemies. David's enemies don't (or won't) believe God can rescue him. He contrasts his enemies' lack of faith with the idea that God protects him, offering him hope of rescue when he cries out to Him. David's confidence is bolstered when God protects him from his enemies, even while resting with his defenses down. Recognizing that victory comes from God and such a victory (hint: a foreshadowing to salvation) blesses God's people, the Psalmist calls on God once more to rescue him and defeat his enemies.

What Does This Imply?

There are people who refuse to recognize God's power, but faith recognizes both God's power and His willingness and ability to protect those who cry out to Him for help. Those who have this faith can rest peacefully—they trust God is watching over them. We can call on God to rescue us from our enemies (physical people, evil, temptations); victory over our them is possible through God. We enjoy victory through a privilege that David did not encounter—Jesus! The cross of Jesus has given us victory though freedom from sin and death and the choice to resist struggles we encounter in our lives. Those who have faith receive the blessing of salvation and through salvation, freedom and security from our enemies.

How are We Invited to Respond?

Each person comes with their own set of struggles. Our struggles or enemies likely look different than an ancient king defending his territory. We might face insecurity, an unforgiving boss, burn out, illness—insert your struggle here. Facing these enemies feels like the odds are stacked against us. Our tangible and intangible enemies may make us question God's power and authority because looking at those difficulties face to face, it's easy to become overwhelmed by the weight of the world and freeze up or shut down. When we feel surrounded by the enemies of our lives, we can do one of three things: 1) Run away from the problem at hand and hope it resolves on its own, 2) Handle the situation on our own and risk burning ourselves out more, or 3) Trust that God is working in cooperation with us and step forward into what we believe is the next good and right thing to do.

In verse 6, David proclaims, "I am not afraid of ten thousand enemies who surround me on every side."

To have faith that God would so surely protect someone from so many enemies is astounding. So is God's ability and willingness to protect one of His children against what looks like impossible odds. But that's what Psalm 3 points us to—victory for God's people, even over sin and death, because Christ has defeated our greatest enemy on the cross. Victory may not happen in every situation and every day. But final, eternal victory is promised for God's believers.

Questions for Reflection

1. What impossible odds do you find yourself facing today?

2. How might God be working in what seems impossible?

Day Two: Psalm 4

What Does This Mean?

The Psalmist calls out to God for help to rescue his reputation. Groundless accusations are thrown at him, and he prays for relief from his distress. Our writer remains hopeful, noting that God treats the godly as set apart, and God will answer his call and take away his distress. The Psalmist is beckoning God to be faithful as part of His covenantal promises to His people.

What Does This Imply?

Anger in and of itself is not sinful. The actions that anger produces can be, but anger without wrongful reaction can be a holy thing. The Psalmist encourages the reader to remain silent so as not to act foolishly. In our silence, we may begin to trust that God sees the situation in full and is willing and able to guide us in situations where someone seeks to harm our reputations.

How are We Invited to Respond?

As insults are being hurled at the Psalmist, I imagine it was tempting to want to throw those insults right back. But the Psalmist's response is to avoid sinning in anger by pausing and thinking about the situation in quiet silence. Is this pausing and thinking a time to let the anger fester and stew? No. That quiet time is meant to lean into trusting God to speak into the situation.

How often have you been insulted and immediately wanted to spring into action with a rebuttal? Instead, the Psalmist advises that we should seek wise counsel in God to help us know how to properly deal with the situation at hand. As God's people, He cares for us. He sees all.

Questions for Reflection

1. What are some of my initial reactions when I am angry?

2. What enables me to quiet myself before God when I am angry and my reputation is attacked?

Day Three: Psalm 5

What Does This Mean?

The Psalmist cries out to the Lord to hear his prayer and acknowledges that God is the only God worth praying to. God does not derive pleasure in wickedness as some do, and those that do will not stand in God's presence. Those who are proud, tell lies, murder, and deceive will not be tolerated in God's Kingdom. But the Psalmist declares his innocence before God because God's mercy is upon him. He begs God to lead him in righteousness and make his path align with God's ways. For those who are faithless, the Psalmist asks that they be destroyed by their own doing. But for those who are faithful, he asks that they be defended. The Psalmist concludes with a request for God to show him how to live through moral actions and characteristics.

What Does This Imply?

It is evident that the Psalmist trusts God to hear his cries for help and that the LORD alone is worthy of taking on the weight of hearing pleas for help. God is set apart as a God who can hear our prayers and, what's more, answer them. God's holiness cannot and will not be sullied by lies, pride, or deception. As a result, people who possess those qualities must either be transformed by God's abundant kindness or be cast away from His presence. God possesses the ability to help a person turn their eyes to Him and His ways by offering wisdom on what is good and right in any given situation. When pressed, will we have the courage to lean into God's wisdom?

How are We Invited to Respond?

Out of God's love, we are welcomed into His presence now and forevermore. But when we face difficult circumstances, we may turn inward and rely on ourselves to make it through. We may turn to characteristics or traits that are not honoring to God. The Psalmist encourages us to cry out to God in times of struggle. The faithful trust that God defends them in their difficulty, and they are formed and shaped in their words, deeds, and actions. The wicked, on the other hand, lie, deceive, and are prideful. They turn away from God until their actions destroy their relationship with Him. In our suffering, we can ask God to shape us morally and in doing so, receive a blessing of joy.

> *"Tell me clearly what to do, which way to turn.*
> *– Psalm 5:8 (TLB)*

Questions for Reflection

1. What are good habits that I can point to that grow my relationship with God? What are bad habits that hinder my relationship with God?

2. Is there a particular moral trait that I sense God might be seeking to develop in me?

Day Four: Psalm 7

What Does This Mean?

God is given an interesting challenge from the Psalmist: tear down the wicked with Your judgement and help those that are obedient. The wicked plot to do harm, but God is just, and therefore, their deeds will have consequences, backfiring on them. Those who are pure of heart are protected. How does the Psalmist propose one can spot the difference between the wicked and the innocent? Only God knows the contents of our minds and hearts; we can trust that God is Protector and Judge.

What Does This Imply?

We learn something significant about God's character here—God is Protector, Judge, Righteous Savior. God does not let evil pass without judgement, and God is able to judge in a way that is perfectly fair. Verse 9 reads, "For you look deep within the mind and heart…" God knows us better than we know our enemies.

Better than we know our friends and family. Better than we know ourselves. God has clarity around situations that we do not. If we are called righteous or unrighteous, God has the authority to do so, though we may plead with Him to see us in a more positive light.

How are We Invited to Respond?

If you've ever been judged unfairly, you know the kind of pain that brings. It may serve as a comfort then to know that God has the authority and ability to judge us and those around us with fairness. If we've been righteous in a situation and the world doesn't see it, God does. God sees the good, the bad, and the ugly within us. And if we get honest with ourselves, we might see glimpses of who we really are, both good and bad. If we are grieving a lack of justice in our lives, we can rest in the fact that nothing goes unseen by God. If others cause us harm, God does not neglect our suffering. If we seek to be declared righteous before God, we must examine our hearts. God looks deep within the contents of our minds and hearts. If we do the same, what will we find? Will we find a heart ready and willing to be continuously transformed by God? Or will we find a heart fixed on something else? Now is the time to prepare ourselves for the day when we all will stand before God and be declared righteous or unrighteous.

Questions for Reflection

1. How well do you believe you know your own heart and mind? How well do you believe you know God's heart and mind? Where do these two areas come together in alignment? In opposition?

2. Is there an area of your life that feels deeply unfair? Where do you believe God might be in the injustice?

Day Five: Psalm 10

What Does This Mean?

The Psalm begins with a question of God: why does it seem like You are far away from Your people? The Psalmist is concerned about those who seem to have no regard for God or others. Godless persons of power plan evil; they lie and murder and are greedy and proud. The hardest part to accept is that they're successful at doing such evil with no apparent thought, care, or fear of God. The evil think they must be untouchable because they prey on the innocent and helpless, who, in turn, collapse. The Psalmist recognizes that God can see the trouble and grief caused by the wicked and invokes God to act justly. God will surely punish those who do wrong, and the helpless must trust that God will justify them.

What Does This Imply?

We live in a world that hasn't fully realized the power and majesty of God. As a result of free will, we may find ourselves facing the consequences of someone else's harmful actions against us. In these circumstances, we might ask God, "are You in this with me?" God knows the full picture of the world before Him in ways we can't even imagine. He sees the ramifications of those who do not honor Him. God means to do something about the injustice in the world, and He means to raise up those who have been harmed, marginalized, or oppressed. God means to bless those the world would traditionally not bless. We know this because if we keep reading our Bibles into the New Testament, Jesus proclaims in the Sermon on the Mount that he means to radically welcome those who have been discarded, marginalized, or otherwise oppressed by the world.

How are We Invited to Respond?

We may find ourselves in one of two boats when reading this Psalm: we are the oppressed or the oppressor. In the case of the oppressed, it is easy to become discouraged when we see someone around us fighting dirty and receiving gain and reward for it. In some cases, we can pursue justice through our actionable intervention (i.e. dialogue, HR reports, our legal system). In other cases, we may feel like sitting ducks. There are some circumstances where only God's intervention can rescue the hurting and hopeless. The Psalmist's response may be helpful in this case: he cries out to God, appealing for His action. (The Psalmist goes so far as to suggest to God, it would be cool if You'd break some arms here so injustice would stop—but I digress). Cry out to God. Ask Him to do something about the situation you find yourself in. He hears the cry of a sighing heart.

In the case of the oppressor, we might think that if God doesn't intervene in the manner we expect, we can hide ourselves and our actions from God. Grace would forgive the wicked if they would only turn back to God's ways. Today, we might not be engaging in political tyranny, but are we aware of those in God's world whom we may be trampling on?

Questions for Reflection

1. Do I find myself existing in the category of oppressed or oppressor?

2. What is my cry to the LORD today?

Day Six: Psalm 12

What Does This Mean?

The Psalmist renders a bitter cry to God as he states the reality of his world. Decency of words and speech has gone out the window. Loyalty and truth aren't valued. Instead, flattery and deception are the norms and all for the sake of personal gain. The Psalmist petitions God to intervene with those who dare to wonder who will stop their wicked ways by silencing their tongues. The Psalmist declares that God's words are true and pure. If God says He will protect, He will. In conclusion, God is faithful to care for the needy (presumably those who are not flattering, deceiving, etc.) against those who are unfaithful to truth.

What Does This Imply?

A pattern in the Psalms may be recognized at this point: there are people who don't recognize God as God. They don't recognize God's lordship, believing that they are the masters of their own lives.

The tongue is a powerful weapon. And yet, even amid wickedness, there are always God's faithful remnant present. These individuals are witnesses to the world regarding God's goodness, and God offers these individuals protection out of God's faithfulness.

How are We Invited to Respond?

When we look at the world around us, we might be discouraged. We may be even more discouraged to see dishonest people succeeding. People may say one thing, but their hearts reveal a different intent. What hope does an honest person have? They have the hope of a God who sees, cares about, and protects the vulnerable. We may choose to be witnesses for good in the world when it would be easier or more profitable to deceive. We may not have the full picture ahead of us, but we can take the next right step of what is good and true. In our lament over the wicked in the world, we can act in opposition by doing the right thing at the most inconvenient time.

Questions for Reflection

1. What does the way I talk reveal about my heart?

2. What does taking the next right step look like in my life?

Day Seven: Psalm 13

What Does This Mean?

The Psalmist opens on a note of despair. He wonders, God, have You forgotten me? We should pay attention to the emphasis of a second question: God, when will You remember me? This is a person in deep pain. David wonders how long he will endure such deep sadness. He imagines that if his suffering continues, it will drive him to the grave, and his enemies will rejoice at his suffering. Continuing in a bold streak, David moves into an invocation to God: ANSWER ME! RESTORE ME! This supplication reads like a persuasive letter: Dear God, I'm in pain, and I'd like You to notice and help me out here. If You answer me, if You restore me, my enemies (the godless ones) will know who You are, God. Protect me from the enemies that gloat about my despair.

The Psalm shifts to a note of deep trust. We might understand verses five through six as saying, God, I trust Your love, and because of that, I know You will rescue me. I will sing Your praises because of Your goodness and faithfulness.

What Does This Imply?

We may be tempted to think that as believers, we will be spared human suffering. Even a favored king (one noted as being a man after God's own heart) knows the crushing sense of despair and the nature of sorrow, suffering, and feeling forgotten. This Psalm shows us that we may approach God boldly with our requests for His intervention and presence in our lives. In our suffering, we may call out to God asking for His restoration. We may ask for protection from those who would rejoice in our defeat. We may also, before we experience rescue, trust that rescue is coming because we trust in God's love and goodness towards us.

How are We Invited to Respond?

In verse three of the Psalm, David says, "Turn and answer me, O LORD my God!" What a bold statement to say to the God of the universe. It's as though David is so confident of his audience before God that he feels a comfortable asking of God boldly when it comes to suffering. We too may ask for God to turn to us in our heartache and remind us that we are not forgotten. We may remember God showing up in our lives in previous circumstances and reflect on what He has transformed, redeemed, and rescued us from. In doing so, we remember God's track record. We must continue to sing His praises because if the rescue hasn't happened yet, our worship is an outward demonstration that we trust that it will. Through Jesus, every believer has been rescued from sin and death. As such, we await an eternity where anguish of the soul ceases. Until that time, we ask God's presence to be with us, and we sing His praises, trusting our rescue from sorrow.

Questions for Reflection

1. What would you have God rescue you from today?

2. Reflect on God's faithfulness in your life.

Day Eight: Psalm 14

What Does This Mean?

The Psalmist describes a notable difference between fallen man's rejection of God and the consequences of such actions and God's faithful followers and the reward of their protection. In the Psalm's context, those who do not recognize God commit evil against God's people. God searches the hearts of the wicked and can find no good within them. Their actions have corrupted them, and they have little regard for their fellow man. The Psalmist notes, the godless will know terror because of their deeds. Though the wicked try to tear away the hope of those faithful believers, they will not succeed. The Psalm concludes with a prophetic word about a Savior who will restore God's people and their oppression will turn to shouts of joy.

What Does This Imply?

Apart from God, goodness is lacking. The LORD knows the condition of our hearts and in the godless, sees corruption. The godless lack the wisdom to know that their "success" will not supersede the plans of God to protect His people. If the foolish knew God, they wouldn't act like they do because they would know of the terror that awaited them. The Jewish people waited for a Savior with hope. Jesus has come to rescue Israel and has initiated restoration on earth. A day is coming when Jesus will return, and all believers will rejoice, for they have known and sought the Lord.

How are We Invited to Respond?

Perhaps you know of someone who is "religious"—they know of God, but they do not regard God as God. If we look in the mirror, we might assess moments in our lives where we are also guilty of this same problem. We might keep sections of our hearts closed off from God when we are in pain, choosing to disregard Him. But the person who disregard's God's active presence in the world is considered a fool. It's difficult to trust someone with the most vulnerable, important, or scarred pieces of ourselves when we have difficulty knowing and relating to them. Part of trusting God is learning to more deeply relate to and engage with God. In doing so, we get the joy of experiencing God's faithfulness. We might also seek wisdom to avoid foolishness. Wisdom may come directly from God, or it may come from people around us who demonstrate trust in the Lord.

Questions for Reflection

1. In what ways am I building my trust in God?

2. Who do I know who could offer Godly wisdom in my life?

Day Nine: Psalm 17

What Does This Mean?

The Psalm begins with urgency—hear me! Listen! Pay attention! Why does the Psalmist want to be heard? Because he feels he's done the right things and is an innocent man, and yet, he has come under fire and is in danger. David declares that God has searched his heart and couldn't find anything amiss in what he says in relation to this particular circumstance. Since David is keeping God's commands, he has avoided a wavering heart. The Psalmist appeals to God's nature and character as the protector of the innocent. David's enemies are ruthless, and they want to see harm come to him. The Psalmist insists upon his vindication from his enemies, and instead of unjust punishment, he desires enjoyment in the presence and protection of God.

What Does This Imply?

Here we have a man who presumably has nothing to hide. There are no cobwebs to be found or embarrassing moments to stumble upon. What you see is what you get! The writer is facing danger, likely as a result of being unwilling to cooperate with corrupt social structures. The Psalmist's enemies have a good thing going—they benefit from corrupt structures, and he is a threat to continued operation. The Psalmist's enemies lack pity because pity would mean they would have to find fault in their actions and change. The Psalmist describes what he believes is an appropriate measure of punishment for his persecutors, going so far as to ask for the corrupt ones' children to experience the same greed his enemies now face. We could argue that the Psalmist is rightfully enraged or that he is horribly hateful and bitter. The Psalm concludes with what could be interpreted as a metaphorical awakening, where he finds satisfaction in eternal presence with God, or a physical awakening, where he finds refreshment with God in a new day where his grievances have been aired.

How are We Invited to Respond?

In verse 14, the Psalmist writes, "Punish them [his enemies] with the sufferings you have stored up for them; may there be enough for their children and some left over for their children's children" (GNT).

When we find ourselves on the moral high ground—when we've been hurt despite doing the right thing—how easy it is to speak and wish harm over the opposing side. This verse reveals a side to the Psalmist's heart that does not demonstrate God's nature.

How do we respond to injustice while not stooping to the same depths as those who do wrong and come after us for doing what is right? We continue to take the next right step of what we believe is good and right. We come to God with our heartaches and complaints and ask that He hears our cries. We must be prepared for God to reveal to us the nature of our own hearts and willing to receive correction if we're not as moral as we'd like to believe ourselves to be.

Questions for Reflection

1. How do we keep our hearts in check to respond righteously to life's circumstances, while also keeping the heart free of a moral superiority complex?

2. What practices/disciplines help us measure the contents of our hearts?

3. What is the nature of your heart today?

Day Ten: Psalm 22

What Does This Mean?

Here, we find the Psalmist feeling abandoned by God. His cries for help go unanswered, despite his persistence. But the Psalmist recognizes, despite his pleas, God is still holy and praise-worthy. God's record of faithfulness throughout human history is proof. The cries of the patriarchs were heard and answered, and God's response did not disappoint.

The author continues, declaring he feels small because of the scorn he receives from his enemies. He is mocked for his reliance on God, who seems distant. The Psalmist asks for God's presence to be near, as God has been near since his birth. Recognizing that he's in the kind of trouble that only God can rescue him from, the Psalmist feels as though he's been left for dead. He is sick and weak, while his enemies are strong.

The Psalm switches from lament to thanksgiving when the Psalmist asks God to be faithful in rescuing him, so the Psalmist can lead his people faithfully. God's rescue will bear witness to God's character: He does not forget the cry of the needy. The people will seek the Lord and return to Him if only the Psalmist would be rescued. The Psalm concludes painting a vision of the earth as a world that knows God and responds in faithfulness because of God delivering the Psalmist. Such witness will impact generations to come.

What Does This Imply?

In this Psalm, we see a picture of a lonely, ill man. The Psalmist demonstrates a level of spiritual maturity in recognizing that despite his feelings and circumstances, the character of God remains holy. The Psalmist rationalizes his logic by stating that the history of God's people is demonstration and witness to God's holiness. The Psalmist is able to know God in the first place because of God's faithfulness to Israel.

As a whole, the Psalm speaks to God's capabilities as a deliverer. The Psalmist recognizes that God alone can deliver him from the kind of trouble he faces. The Psalmist's role in deliverance is to bear witness and testimony to God's faithfulness. This would enable others in God's kingdom to praise God and know God more deeply, too.

How are We Invited to Respond?

We may be inclined to turn away and isolate ourselves from the face of God when we feel God isn't answering our prayers in a timely manner or in the ways we think they should be answered. However, in 22:3 (ESV), the Psalmist makes an important statement: "Yet you are holy." Even when the Psalmist feels ignored and alone, he determines that God's nature isn't impacted by human circumstances. The author trusts that God isn't limited by human constraints, and so, God will not always ignore his cry.

When we lament feeling forgotten in hard circumstances, we might consider:

1. Asking God why. We may learn something about who God is. In verses 16–18, we may note that Jesus echoed some of these words on the cross. In crying out to God, we depend on Him and seek to know God's face.

2. Remembering God is bigger than our circumstances.

3. Continuing to pray for deliverance. Our words have spiritual impact. Likewise, we may be encouraged to remember that if deliverance doesn't happen in this life, Christ has made a way that our deliverance is guaranteed, not just for a lifetime but for eternity. Christ died on a cross and was abandoned by God so that we would not have to be.

4. Upon deliverance, giving testimony to others to bear witness to a God who has heard the cry of the needy.

Questions for Reflection

1. What reaction do you have to the idea that Christ died abandoned and alone so that we wouldn't have to?

2. What prayer for deliverance can you pray boldly before God today?

Day Eleven: Psalm 25

What Does This Mean?

The Psalmist begins, "O LORD, I give my life to you. I trust in you, my God!" (Psalm 25:1–2). The author's eyes are fixed on God, and yet, he has committed sins in his youth, and it's coming back to bite him. The Psalmist has enemies who are likely making a mockery of him for youthful indiscretions. And so, the Psalmist asks God to guide him in truth, trusting that God will save him because God has done it time and time again.

The Psalm switches from personal narrative to a generalized audience of those who have faith in God and occasionally transgress (can we relate?). The Psalmist suggests that God's character teaches sinners what is good and right, leading the meek and poor to Him.

Once more, the Psalmist implores God to forgive his sins because such forgiveness will be a demonstration of God staying true to His nature and character. God is described as One who delivers those who keep their eyes on Him and helps those who seek Him to escape temptation.

The Psalm concludes with an appeal for rescue and recognizes that, though the Psalmist is an imperfect person, God is faithful and will protect him because it's part of God's nature.

What Does This Imply?

Those who fear the LORD live in prosperity, not because trials or sins are erased from all memory or have no repercussions but because their spirits' can be at ease due to a close relationship with God.

As Romans 8:1 (KJV) depicts, "There is therefore now no condemnation to them which are in Christ Jesus, who walk not after the flesh, but after the Spirit." Those who keep their eyes on the LORD, even imperfectly, may enjoy close relationship to God as protector. Through God's character, we may learn what is good, right, and wise, growing from the follies of youth. David would have understood the receiving of God's wisdom through knowing and understanding God's laws. Today, we understand what is good, right, and wise through the model and life of Jesus and his gift to the church—the Holy Spirit.

How are We Invited to Respond?

There is a unique kind of lament in the soul when we know we've messed up. Such laments often show up as shame and guilt. In this Psalm, the author expresses remorse for the sins of his youth. We have a name for this practice: confession. Augustine of Hippo noted that, "The confession of evil works is the first beginning of good works."[3] The spiritual discipline of confession changes us objectively to be in relationship with God.[4] Confession can be done individually and corporately where we cooperate with God's will and cooperate in strengthening others to do the same. In confessing, we take responsibility for our actions and express sorrow, examine our conscience, and release the penalty of sin to God. We come to God with specific sins on our hearts and are set free from the bounds of our sin, so we can turn away from it and continue doing good.[5] We ask for God's aid in helping us live more holy lives. When we know we are forgiven, we move to celebration as we rejoice in our freedom and connection with God. The sins of youth are forgotten by a changed life and a merciful God.

Once we are made aware of our own sinfulness, it also becomes more difficult to condemn others for their sins.

Questions for Reflection

1. Are you holding onto shame or guilt that can be confessed and released to God today?

2. What does celebration of your freedom in forgiveness look like practically?

Day Twelve: Psalm 26

What Does This Mean?

"Declare me innocent, O LORD, for I have acted with integrity; I have trusted in the LORD without wavering" (Psalm 26:1). The Psalmist starts off on a bold note. The writer asks for his innocence to be declared because his actions have demonstrated integrity. His trust in God has been unwavering. The Psalmist goes so far as to ask God to put him on trial and examine him so that the LORD will see him living according to the truth (it is helpful to interpret this as the Law).

One might imagine the Psalmist telling God, I don't spend time around the kinds of people who would shape my life away from You. I don't do what the wicked do. I don't hang out with people who set their minds on empty things or people who say they are religious but really aren't and especially not those who totally disregard my faith!

The author continues, I love to be in the house of the LORD because there I can delight in God's presence. Because of this very compelling case that I've made to You, God, don't give me, an innocent man, the same punishment or fate as murderers, those who scheme, the wicked, etc., because I am innocent, God! I don't do what the wicked do. Save me, God, and I will praise You for it.

Why Does This Imply?

The Psalmist makes an interesting claim: I am wholeheartedly innocent, God! So, please, save me! A Christian understanding of humanity is that all have fallen short of God's glory. No one, not one person, is righteous (Romans 3:10). In this Psalm's context, the Psalmist is making an appeal for his innocence because he has explicitly followed God's laws. He has not tempted himself away from God's laws by associating with the wicked. He has washed his hands of unrighteousness. Because he has physically separated himself from spiritually poor company, the Psalmist believes that suffering the same fate as the wicked isn't fair or just. The Psalmist appeals to God's just nature as the reason he should be saved. Because God saves the Psalmist, he will offer praise and thanksgiving in worship.

How are We Invited to Respond?

"Don't let me suffer the fate of sinners" (Psalm 26:9). The Psalmist has created a dichotomy in his head: me vs the sinners. We in the church may be tempted with the same mentality. Yet, we all stand as sinners. The laws that the Psalmist states he follows could not deliver us from sin but hold up a mirror to our sin (Romans 3:20). The Deliverer of our sin, the great Vindicator, and our Advocate is God With Us—Jesus Christ. Apart from Christ, we all would suffer the fate of sinners.

Christ associated with those the world called sinners: the prostitutes, the bribe accepters, the shameful. Jesus made a tax collector one of his own disciples! We must give pause before considering our works before God as what make us innocent. Our innocence is through Christ taking on the penalty of our guilt and welcoming us into radical mercy. Our innocence is through faith that Christ has made it so. And through the gift of our salvation, we may respond with our praise and worship. We may also seek to welcome the "guilty" into "innocence" through our witness and testimony of God's great love.

Questions for Reflection

1. What are some inward or outward responses to receiving the gift of salvation? Do you find yourself regularly expressing these?

2. John Wesley invited the Methodists to ask themselves this regularly: "Am I consciously or unconsciously creating the impression that I am better than I really am? In other words, am I a hypocrite?"[6]

Day Thirteen: Psalm 27

What Does This Mean?

The Psalmist opens with a reflection that he need not be afraid because God has a track record of protecting him. The author is confident that his enemies will not thwart him because God cares for him. The Psalmist asks God to enable him access to God's presence for all his days. Access to God's presence means he will delight in deliverance from his enemies, and for his deliverance, the Psalmist will praise God.

Verse 7 transitions us into a lament. The Psalmist pleads for God's mercy because his enemies plot against him. He wrestles between the lines of heartache for his situation and his certainty of God's care for him. The author notes that he's been abandoned by those closest to him and asks God to teach him how to live honestly. In doing so, he may avoid demise under false accusations made by his enemies. The Psalmist trusts that God will answer him, and he will experience God's favor.

What Does This Imply?

We seem to have two different themes appearing in this Psalm: thanksgiving *and* lament. Scholars believe that Psalm 27 may have been two psalms at one time.[7] Thanksgiving and lament may feel counterintuitive, but the common link between the two is faith. In verses 1–6, the Psalmist connects God's presence to safety and delight. Faith is required to recognize that God's power can bring about such things. Verses 7–14 wrestle with lament, while the Psalmist has faith that God will see him through false accusations. By living honestly, the Psalmist may know God's goodness. By faith, the author can receive God's goodness.

How are We Invited to Respond?

> *"Even if my father and mother abandon me, the LORD will hold me close." – Psalm 27:10*

The Psalmist's closest loved ones have abandoned him in his trouble, but he has the faith to know that God has not abandoned him. We may be tempted in times of difficulty to believe that God has left us. But Scripture declares that God is near to the broken-hearted (Psalm 34:18). When we feel abandoned by those around us, God has not abandoned us. When the floor falls out from under us, if we would keep our eyes on Him, we encounter the presence of the LORD instead of running from it. This Psalm teaches us that we can pray for God's presence to be with us in times of distress. We can also ask God to help us to know how to walk in paths of honesty and avoid further peril.

Questions for Reflection

1. Do you have any circumstances in your life that feel so troublesome that you feel isolated and alone in carrying them?

2. Read Matthew 11:28–30. How does Jesus help us carry our burdens?

3. Consider a past or current adverse circumstance in your life. Have you ever felt abandoned by God? Read Psalm 34:18. Go to God in prayer, asking Him to heal your sense of abandonment and reveal truth to you. Sit quietly, allowing God to speak to you. If this is a new practice for you, try setting a five-minute timer.

Day Fourteen: Psalm 28

What Does This Mean?

At this point, perhaps you've picked up on a pattern—the Psalmist's work often begins with a cry to the LORD. The Psalmist offers God a name we should notice: the rock. The author pleads, don't be deaf to my call for help because if You ignore me, I might as well be dead. The Psalmist doesn't think he stands a fighting chance against his enemies because he is weak, so he lifts his hands to God in an appeal for help. He begs God to help him avoid meeting the same fate as the wicked. Though his enemies on a surface level appear friendly, they are wicked at heart. The Psalmist calls on God to justly punish the wicked for their deeds. We see a kind of eye for an eye approach pop up. The Psalmist argues, these enemies of mine don't care about the LORD, so God, tear them down!

The Psalm takes a shift at verse 6. The Psalmist's prayers have been answered. God has heard the author's cry for help. The

Psalmist affirms trust in God and offers praise and thanksgiving. The author finishes the Psalm with an invocation: God, continue to protect and bless Your people.

What Does This Imply?

The Psalmist offers a combination of trust and humanity in his words. Though he calls on the LORD to be his rock against his enemies, he also seeks to make a verdict of judgement on his enemies. In proclaiming a harsh penalty towards his enemies, we see an angry, hurt human being. As the prayer shifts, we see that once again, God has been faithful in answering the cry of the needy. God has delivered the Psalmist. God's faithfulness is evidenced and witnessed through the author's praise and thanksgiving.

How are We Invited to Respond?

We should remember that the Psalms are a collection of written works that capture the full range of human emotion. Some emotions are holier than others. We would be wise to reflect on whether or not the Psalmist's emotions come from holiness or humanity. It's incredible that God would utilize a collection of emotional poetry to repeatedly demonstrate that God shows up faithfully. When David asks God to condemn his enemies, it acts in opposition to Christ's call to love our enemies. David's words are coming from an outpouring of emotion. To be sure, employing justice is integral to the nature and character of God. But when we've been hurt and are lamenting, we must seek accountability in others to the extent that it reforms not destroys them. God's version of accountability seeks to draw people closer to Him.

If part of your lament today is because of harm from another person, a thoughtful idea emerges in the final verses of this Psalm, verses 6–9:

1. Trust in God to deliver us from our circumstances against those who harm or seek to harm us.

2. In trusting, we position ourselves for help through faith.

3. We praise God as witnesses to God's faithfulness (this specific Psalm seems to indicate worship through song).

Questions for Reflection

1. Take a moment to write down something(s) that you seek God's help in. Pray your request(s) daily. Come back to this list in a month and consider God's faithfulness in answering our prayers.

2. Is the accountability you offer restorative or destructive?

Day Fifteen: Psalm 31

What Does This Mean?

The Psalmist knows what it is to feel endangered. The Psalmist knows what it is to be ill. The Psalmist knows what it is to be a social pariah. Today's Psalm is a three-for-one deal on lament. In our opening, the Psalmist seeks protection from danger that is impending. He asks for God's help in rescuing him from enemy traps. The Psalmist compares and emphasizes the trust he has in God for deliverance with the trust his enemies place in their false gods.

Verse 9 starts a new idea: a lament for illness. The suffering the Psalmist has endured is eating at him, heart, mind, and body. He feels forgotten and shunned by those around him; even his friends avoid him. The Psalmist has suffered for some time and wastes away because of it.

Verse 13 suggests more danger lurks for the Psalmist in whispers around town. He calls on God's rescue for the preservation of his life and notes that God should judge the Psalmist favorably and show mercy, but the wicked should be disgraced and silenced.

A final shift occurs in the Psalm to what appears to be the joy and thanksgiving felt because of answered prayers. God has protected. God has sheltered. God has blessed. Just when the Psalmist thought it was all over, God showed up. The Psalm closes with a call to love God because of His protection, encouraging others who wait for deliverance to have courage because the LORD is coming.

What Does This Imply?

This is a Psalm that speaks to the very real highs and lows we have in life. The Psalmist both asks for God's protection and remembers to trust that God rescues. In prayer, we might start with an ask and in the process remember God's faithfulness. We might begin to trust that God is already working in our circumstances.

When the Psalmist commits his spirit to God, he is faced with what we all must face: God is responsible for the soul and its place upon death. The Psalmist expresses a readiness to meet his maker. His grief is so severe that it confines him to the extent that he feels isolated as he ponders the depths of his sorrow. And yet, he trusts in God. Such an expression of trust grants him flickers of hope and joy that he will be delivered from his circumstances. His trust is a call for help and confidence in God to deliver. The Psalmist is reminded of who is in control and urges others to trust and hope so that they may experience the Psalmist's joy.

How are We Invited to Respond?

Psalm 31 may have been created as a general catch all for the person/communities who seek God in suffering. Perhaps the events of this Psalm didn't take place chronologically, but in life, suffering can stack up, sometimes hitting us all at once. When suffering rains, it pours.

One of the circumstances the Psalmist mentions might be enough to break a person, but everything he lists? Crushing.

Let the words of the Psalmist comfort you. Just when it seems to be all over, God shows up. Just when we think we can't handle our hurt and grief anymore, God shows up.

The Psalm closes with, "Be strong, and let your heart take courage, all you who wait for the LORD!" (Psalm 31:24 ESV). To be strong, to let our hearts take courage, we must hold onto hope. Hope gives us the strength and conviction to have faith that something better awaits us. We may be fortunate enough to see our hope transpire in this life, but we are guaranteed to see the fruit of hope in eternity. That is because we love a God who has ultimately, permanently chosen to show up. Find hope in that today.

Questions for Reflection

1. Is there an area in your life that feels hopeless? What would it be like to experience hope in this area?

2. How does God heal our hurts?

3. What is a practical, tangible way that your heart can take new courage in the LORD today?

Day Sixteen: Psalm 36

What Does This Mean?

The Psalmist begins that those who have no fear of God are blind to sin. Sin whispers to the unbeliever, and they cannot comprehend their own wickedness. Their words and actions are blinded by sin, and they make no attempt to turn from evil.

The Psalm pivots from a picture of one who walks in sin to one who is guided by God. The sinful one is restricted to sin, the godly delight in the boundless love of God. The Psalmist describes a God of righteousness and justice. God cares for creation, providing shelter, food, and drink (related to both physical and spiritual needs, but particular emphasis is given here on the spiritual).

The Psalm concludes: "Pour out your unfailing love on those who love you; give justice to those with honest hearts" (Psalm 36:10). The Psalmist reflects that it is only a matter of time before the wicked will fall.

What Does This Imply?

It may be that the first half of the Psalm reflects on the nature of a person before they became a believer, and the Psalm transitions to a spiritual awakening of one who encounters God for themselves. It may also be that this Psalm juxtaposes two different people: the one who lives according to sin and the one who lives according to grace.

The Psalmist reflects that the wicked make no attempt to turn from evil. Those bound to their sin are so entrenched in wickedness that they cannot clearly see who and what they've become. The wicked cannot comprehend of a God who can rescue because in their minds, there is no need for rescue in the first place. As the Psalmist delves into a picture of what it is to know God, we get a sense of a different life than the one in verses 1–4. The godly have their eyes opened; they can see unfailing love, righteousness, and justice. Those who know God can witness God's providence in creation and rejoice!

The Psalmist contemplates the fate of the wicked. There is a time when the wicked and their plans will not succeed against the godly. It is in this knowledge that we can believe that God pours out His unfailing love on those who love Him.

How are We Invited to Respond?

Have you ever felt trampled by another person? One who takes advantage of every situation they can for their personal gain? It's a discouraging feeling because we seek to honor God with our lives by doing the right thing, even if it doesn't get us ahead. The words of this Psalm help point us in the right direction of where we keep our focus. When the wicked are being wicked, we recount God's unfailing love towards us. We think about the depths to which God has reached out to us and been faithful in restoring us. We remember that God's justice and righteousness prevails against the wicked and that God cares for His people. When we are weak, we may call upon Him to provide us with spiritual food and drink to nourish our souls and help us through another day. If you're unfamiliar with the idea of spiritual disciplines, I invite you to look up Richard Foster's work. His writing gives practical tools for how a person can partake in spiritual nourishment (i.e. prayer, quiet time, worship, etc.).

Call upon the LORD in prayer with the words, "Pour out your unfailing love on those who love you; give justice to those with honest hearts. Don't let the proud trample me or the wicked push me around" (Psalm 36:10–11).

Questions for Reflection

1. Where have you seen God's love pouring out for you?

2. Pray, "Pour out your unfailing love on those who love you; give justice to those with honest hearts. Don't let the proud trample me or the wicked push me around" (Psalm 36:10–11).

Day Seventeen: Psalm 39

What Does This Mean?

We learn an important lesson in this Psalm: the tongue is a powerful weapon. The Psalmist begins by recognizing that complaining in the presence of the non-religious is damaging to the witness of God and their own potential faith. But alone, the Psalmist's silence grows unbearable. His thoughts consume and burn him to the extent that he can no longer hold back.

The Psalmist's depression is evident as he writes that life is short and fleeting. The author compares human existence to the insubstantial and worthless. He stipulates that his life is all for nothing. Where can he find hope? In God alone. Only God can rescue our author from his sin. The Psalmist stands quietly before God because he submits himself in obedience to God; he will not continue the pattern of his sin.

The Psalmist calls upon God to provide relief because his problems are a result of his own sin. In providing relief, God ensures that the Psalmist will no longer appear a fool for his mistakes or be crushed from the penalty of his offence. The Psalm concludes with a plea to hear the Psalmist's prayers and cries. He invokes God's protection as a sojourner, one who culturally was granted liberties of special consideration and hospitality. The author's plea is this: spare me from Your anger so that I can experience gladness before I die.

What Does This Imply?

Our Psalmist expresses concern with how he speaks around those who do not share in his faith. We might also give care and consideration for how we speak of our frustrations around those who do not share our faith so as not to discourage potential development of their faith. If in good times we proclaim a God of goodness but in difficult times we offer complaints, how do we bear witness to the nature and character of God?

This Psalm also serves as a reminder of the weight of sin and how our choices can crush us. Sin would leave us in shame and exhaustion with the sense that life is meaningless. However, because our hope is in the LORD, we stand forgiven by His grace. Life isn't withering away—it is made new by the blood of Jesus. Life isn't short or temporal but eternal.

When God extends forgiveness for our sins, we are treated with the hospitality of one being welcomed into God's Kingdom.

How are We Invited to Respond?

The Psalmist writes, "I am silent before you; I won't say a word, for my punishment is from you" (Psalm 39:9).

This suggests that the Psalmist's sin was speaking out of turn against God. The Psalmist recognizes his sin and changes direction. The Psalmist is silent before God to demonstrate how he is refocusing on God and turning away from sin. The punishment the Psalmist speaks of is a conviction and consequence of sin brought on by the Psalmist's choices.

We can see this Psalm as a process of repentance.

1. We too can recognize the weight of our sin and experience its consequences (a form of lament, no doubt.)

2. We may hope in the LORD and ask for God's deliverance.

3. We may turn towards God by seeking His presence and changing our actions to demonstrate a willingness to turn away from sin.

4. We may be welcomed into God's Kingdom, having received the LORD's hospitality as forgiven and reconciled persons.

Questions for Reflection

1. How does silence before God create space for obedience?

2. God knows our hearts better than we do. What does it say about the nature and character of God that He would invite us into redemption?

Day Eighteen:
Psalm 40:12-17

What Does This Mean?

When reading Psalm 40, it can feel like we are reading two psalms. Verses 1–11 seem to indicate a psalm of thanksgiving as a result of healing from sickness. Verse 12 acts as a transition verse into a psalm of lament. The Psalmist wrestles with consequences from his sin in verse 12, but in verse 13, he details sins committed or about to be committed by enemies. Verse 13 asks God's quick help to prevent the author's destruction and humiliation. He describes two categories of people: those delighting in his trouble, who should experience the shame they wish upon him (presumably non-believers) and those who search for God and should be filled with joy and gladness (presumably believers). The Psalm ends with confidence—God is with me as helper and savior.

What Does This Imply?

We might consider that a person who has wrestled significantly with illness would be vulnerable and exhausted. Here, the author reflects on the overwhelming nature of his own sin and its consequences for life. With too many troubles to count, he is discouraged. On top of that, the Psalmist is pursued by those who seek to humiliate him. This is a low place to be. Implicitly, he may believe that, despite all that is taking place, in searching for God, he may be filled with joy again. Despite his state as needy and poor, the Psalmist believes that the LORD still has him on the radar. God is helper and deliverer. For a man who is tired and potentially in danger, it is unsurprising that he would remark, deliver me quickly, God!

How are We Invited to Respond?

"But may all who search for you be filled with joy and gladness in you." – Psalm 40:16

Those who seek God find joy and gladness because to encounter God, particularly when life isn't going well, is to have the chance to exult and worship Him properly. In worshipping God, we find joy because we remember who He is and are delighted because of it. To be filled with joy is to place God in His proper place, where we are reminded of our confidence in His qualities as helper and deliverer. We rely less on our circumstances to make it through the drudgery of life, we seek God, and we are filled with gladness because through Him, we are helped. We are saved. Amen!

Questions for Reflection

1. In my daily life, how do I seek to glorify God?

2. Do I trust that God is working beyond the limitations of my circumstances?

3. Reflect on this Scripture from Isaiah 41:13 (NIV), "For I am the LORD your God who takes hold of your right hand and says to you, Do not fear; I will help you."

Day Nineteen: Psalm 41

What Does This Mean?

This Psalm is composed of equal parts lament and reflection, considering the author's deliverance from illness. Verses 1–3 consider God's rescue and protection.

In verse 4, the author switches from broad statements to an autobiographical account of his life. The Psalmist relays how he has seen God involved throughout his illness. We get a sense that when he was ill, there were people preparing for his death. The author's closest friend contributed to the gossip mill about his illness. In verse 10, the Psalmist appeals to God's mercy. The author's humanity is made clear when he states, God, make me well so that I can get back at those who have betrayed me!

The Psalm wraps up on a more victorious note. Illness will not get the last word, and neither will the plots of the enemy. A doxology is offered in closing Book One of the Psalms.

What Does This Imply?

This Psalm offers a glimpse of the power of hindsight. The Psalmist begins this text describing his illness as a reflection of how God moved in his life during a difficult time. Would he note the same wisdom at the beginning or in the thick of illness? It's difficult to say. As the author moves away from generalizations in the opening, we gain insight into how low of a circumstance the Psalmist had faced. It may be that on his sickbed his visitors began to gossip about his demise. A dear friend may have broken his confidence and relayed too much information to too many people or the wrong person. A powerful sting, indeed. The Psalmist asks for healing to pay back his enemies. This serves as a reminder that just because something is written in Scripture doesn't mean a particular figure's behavior or action is right.

How are We Invited to Respond?

No form of betrayal is kind to the heart, but a betrayal by a friend or loved one that hits close to home wreaks devastation and confusion. We should be wary of reading this Psalm and deciding it is wise to ask God to help us through our difficult circumstances for the sake of getting back at those who have not helped us along the way. To do so acts in opposition to the model of Christ. Human response may naturally be inclined to want to pay back, but Jesus' response is to turn the other cheek. We may be prone to shy away from this modest and humble response to those who do us harm. How will justice be served? How will the wrong be made right? We must trust that God sees injustice and is actively working to create a world where all wrongs will be righted and injustice will no longer be a part of His good creation.

Questions for Reflection

1. Read Matthew 5:38-39 (NIV): "'You have heard that it was said, 'Eye for eye, and tooth for tooth.' But I tell you, do not resist an evil person. If anyone slaps you on the right cheek, turn to them the other cheek also.'" Is it your natural disposition to turn the other cheek or put up a fight?

2. How has hindsight been a part of your faith development?

Day Twenty: Psalm 42

What Does This Mean?

As we read this Psalm, we might see a relatable theme emerge—loneliness. Our author begins seeking relief from God as a deer seeks relief from thirst by drinking water. The author longs for God's company as one removed from their home and place of worship. Even away from home base, he is unable to escape taunts from enemies.

The author remembers good days of being in community with others, worshipping God, and celebrating God's presence. With such memories fresh in his mind, the Psalmist wrestles with two ideas. On the one hand, he has experienced deep joy, so he wonders why he is sad and discouraged. On the other hand, he is lonely and longs to know God's presence. The Psalmist resolves to hope in God that better days are ahead.

In verse 6, the Psalmist continues his self-consolation. He notes, I'm still discouraged, and yet, God's presence is evident in my life's history. So, the author remembers God's love poured out and continues his prayers to seek and find God. He cries out, remembering God's faithfulness, asking if God remembers him. Our poet has been wandering in darkness, pursued by enemies and mocked. His enemies even mock God, asking if God has forgotten the Psalmist too. The Psalm closes with the author hoping in God, worshipping Him as Savior.

What Does This Imply?

The Psalm wrestles with the tension of human mood and perspective. It begins on a somber note, reflects on joyful times, crashes back into depression, and ends on a hopeful note. We experience some emotional whiplash here!

In the Psalmist's loneliness, it is hard for him to see God's presence, but he is consoled by remembering happier times. We may note that the mind's thoughts offer a powerful directive. Memory sets the Psalmist on the right track, away from despair, but this act isn't quite enough to solve the problem of loneliness. It is when he remembers God's historic witness of love in his life that the mood of the Psalm picks up.

The Psalm concludes with resolute determination: I will hope in God because I know God will save because He has done it before.

How are We Invited to Respond?

One of the ways that loneliness occurs is when we reflect on the gift of community and better days, longing for them again. Our memories serve as a powerful reminder of how we know and understand God. How we frame our memories can dig us into deeper depression or dig us out of hopelessness. In the Psalmist's loneliness, he remembers God's love throughout his life and reflects on how His love has shown up visibly (through geography and creation). The Psalmist's loneliness doesn't evaporate into thin air in this Psalm. Ours may not either. However, his mood changes as a result of remembering the nature and character of God. The load of loneliness becomes less burdensome when we can hope in God's rescue because we can point to how we've been rescued before.

Questions for Reflection

1. In what circumstance(s) has God poured out His loving kindness to you?

2. How easy or difficult is it for you to process your memories with a lens of hope?

Day Twenty-One: Psalm 43

What Does This Mean?

It is possible that Psalm 43 is a continuation of Psalm 42.[8] However, rather than focusing on loneliness, this psalm emphasizes injustice. The Psalmist asks God to defend against the ungodly and liars. He recognizes that God alone can keep him safe, but he wonders if the Lord has tossed him aside. He feels as though he's walking blind in the midst of his enemies.

Verse 3 switches tone from unstable despair to rational processing. He articulates, God, send Your light and truth, and surely, I'll be safe in Your presence. Verse 5 offers the same question asked in Psalm 42, "Why am I discouraged?" With rationality and reason restored, the Psalmist is saying, with what I know of God, why would I be discouraged? Why would I be sad? I will hope in God because I know who God is, and I will praise God for it!

What Does This Imply?

In the face of injustice, our Psalmist has become a bit unhinged. He begs God to be vindicated and freed from injustice. His soul is in such turmoil that he asks God, where are You? When will You show up?

The mood shifts when the Psalmist pauses to consider the circumstances at hand. He asks God to send out His light and truth. God's light is meant to describe His face turned favorably toward the Psalmist. His truth is a description of God's character. And so, the Psalmist is asking that God's presence be with him and that He would make truth known. To be taken to the mountains is another symbol of being in God's presence.

When the Psalmist asks, "why am I discouraged?" (Psalm 43:5), we see a person who has let their faith supersede their feelings and circumstances. In doing so, he remembers and sees God more clearly as One who will deliver. God's got me, he remembers, because that's just who He is. And so, worship of God flows out of knowing God.

How are We Invited to Respond?

When the Psalmist asks God, "Why have you tossed me aside?" (Psalm 43:2), his language suggests that out of anger, God has rejected the Psalmist. God has left the Psalmist to figure out his situation for himself. That's a common human response, isn't it? We ask, God, where are You in my hurt? Where are You in my suffering? Are You just going to leave me here alone to figure this out?

No. God promises not to leave or forsake us. He promises to be near to the brokenhearted. But it certainly doesn't always feel that way. We would be wise not to set aside what we know is the truth about God for our feelings, particularly when life feels unstable.

We must remember who God is and how He has been faithful and invite His presence and truth to be revealed to us so that we may have the confidence of the Psalmist to say, "I will put my hope in God" (Psalm 43:5).

Questions for Reflection

1. How easy or difficult is it for you to trust that God has not left or forsaken you?

2. What area of your life are you asking God, when will You show up?

3. Take a moment to go to God in prayer. Ask God to reveal how He is working in your life in ways you may not see. Allow time to listen to the LORD's leading.

Day Twenty-Two: Psalm 52

What Does This Mean?

To better understand the context of Psalm 52, it's helpful to share another Bible story first.

In Israel's history, the people specifically requested a king. Eventually, God relented and gave the people King Saul. But Saul began to disobey God, and a powerful movement emerged where the people wanted a new king. The man for the job? David. Saul was so enraged by the idea that he could be replaced that David had to go into hiding to preserve his life.

Psalm 52 details a story found in 1 Samuel where David hides with a priest named Ahimelech until he moves on to a cave. A man named Doeg, the Edomite, spies David with Ahimelech, and Ahimelech is summoned before King Saul to be asked about David's whereabouts. Saul orders Doeg to kill Ahimelech when he refuses to reveal information about David. Doeg honors the king's wishes and kills not just Ahimelech but also Ahimelech's associates. It's bloody and many innocent people die. David is made aware of Saul's actions because Ahimelech's son, Abiathar, escapes death and finds David. Because of the horrifying news, David realizes the kind of king Saul is and accepts God's role for him as the future king of Israel (for the full story, see 1 Samuel 22).

Psalm 52 is written in response to the gruesome actions of Doeg and King Saul. Scholars disagree on whom the Psalm is explicitly directed at, whether Doeg, King Saul, or general enemies that include the aforementioned parties. Either way, in this Psalm, we see a man shouting against his adversary/adversaries.

The Psalmist writes that his enemy has harmed, not helped, God's people and should be mindful about boasting of his actions. The author's enemy is hit with the following insults: liar and traitor. The enemy is accused of betraying God's people because he loves evil and lying more than what is true.

But the enemy's time is coming. His evil will not last. He will be removed from power and lose influence and wealth. The interesting thing to note is that God will be the One removing these things. When the righteous see all that the enemy has lost, they will laugh at those who believed in evil, trivial things more than they believed in God.

Those who trust in God's love will flourish like an olive tree (which happens to be a very fruitful plant). Godly people (in which the Psalmist includes himself) will praise God because they know that the blessings they have come from God.

What Does This Imply?

The Psalm could relate to general enemies but could also address a very specific enemy of our author. Either way, our Psalmist seeks revolution where the misdeeds of the wicked and the liars will be seen and noted. The evil will be removed from authority. Clarity will arise for the wicked and the righteous. Those who trusted in their wealth and power will come to see just how poor they were. Those who trusted in God will see they are wealthy in the fruitfulness given by Him. The righteous will come out on top because of and through God's mercies. Since they know where they have received their flourishing, they will worship and honor God.

How are We Invited to Respond?

Take a moment to imagine being in David's shoes. He's been on the run from a crazy king trying to kill him because others are saying he should be the next king. While on the run, he sees the son of the man who took him in during a desperate time, only to find out that as a result of his generosity, he's been killed.

Can you imagine the kind of grief and anger that would stir up within you? Maybe a sense of injustice? And maybe just a hint of conviction that it was time to step in so that this kind of thing wouldn't happen again?

It may be a little hard to put yourself in David's shoes, but there are moments in each of our lives when we come across something that doesn't sit right with us. We know something is wrong. Maybe we don't know what to do about it, or maybe we do, but it will require a significant amount of courage to act on it.

Lament is not an uncommon response to injustice. Lament tells us that something is amiss in a world that was initially designed to be better. Our sense of revolution might not be to the same level and degree that David encountered, but it might look like doing something to make sure the wrong doesn't happen again. It may mean speaking up and acting in a way that is particular to our roles, gifts, and contexts to uplift the righteous. God invites us into a mission of redemption for the world.

Here's what Psalm 52 tells us: those who trust in God's love will flourish like an olive tree. Those who know of God's love, believe in His love to transform, and obey His loving wisdom for creation will flourish, not because of what we've done but because of who God is. I won't promise that the flourishing will start today, but I can say that if it doesn't happen in this lifetime, I'd rather have eighty hard years of correcting injustice for the world than an eternity away from justice. We can't ignore what we can help restore.

Questions for Reflection

1. What role do you play and what gifts do you have that aid in revolutionizing the world into a place that reflects God's goodness?

2. Can you recall a time when God enabled you to flourish amid hardship?

Day Twenty-Three: Psalm 53

What Does This Mean?

This Psalm acts as a kind of prophetic warning to what will become of the wicked upon God's deliverance of His people. Opening with a caricature of the godless, the Psalmist describes the fool as one who fails to recognize God's tangible presence and acts corruptly as a result. The author imagines God looking down on His people to see if anyone has wisdom, but He can't find a single person. All have fallen away from God.

The Psalmist asks, won't these people ever understand how things really work? The wicked devour the Israelites but wouldn't think to call upon God's name. The Psalmist pictures the death of a corrupt generation. Before long, heretics and apostates of the time will know the terror of their ways. God will break their bones and reject them from His presence.

The Psalmist changes the tone of the Psalm with a cry for the day that God will come to Mount Zion and rescue His people.

What Does This Imply?

Our Psalmist is greatly disturbed by the deadened faith in his community. He notes that those who do not or will not know God are fools, and such foolishness enables them to act corruptly. The Psalmist's language indicates something shocking: all have turned away from God as He sought someone with understanding. No one is capable of real understanding. If understanding were revealed *and* understood, humanity would not be dealing with so much corruption. God's search to find a wise person illustrates the severity of the problem. The Psalmist thinks God should take action. He insists that the corrupt should all be destroyed! Can you imagine the terror of being destroyed and sent away from God's presence?

Our Psalmist is so worked up by the problem of wickedness that he forgets that there are still some good people of faith left. All hope may not be lost. The Psalmist longs for and prophesies about a day where God's people are restored. Restoration in this context translates to being healed and rescued from sin and corruption.

How are We Invited to Respond?

Verse 6 notes, "When God restores his people," and with the text, a prophetic word emerges—may God rescue us from our own foolishness and evil. The Psalmist's verdict for the wicked is clear: humanity is corrupt, and God should crush some bones and call it a good day. And yet, we know that God did not give up on humanity. Instead, God gave His only Son so that we would be rescued from our foolishness and corruption.

When we mourn the state of the world around us, we might also consider God's mercy on humanity, remembering that He seeks to restore us. Even believers have fallen short of understanding God and acting accordingly. Such recognition may prompt us to remember that we have a God who seeks after the corrupt because it is possible that they will be transformed into what is good and holy. May we willingly seek transformation and participate in helping to heal a hurting world to demonstrate to the fools that God cannot and will not be ignored.

Questions for Reflection

1. When are you most inclined to recognize God's mercy in your life? Least?

2. How does the knowledge of our own corruption change how we look at those we view as corrupt?

Day Twenty-Four: Psalm 54

What Does This Mean?

Have you ever been in a situation where you feel helpless? That's the position our Psalmist is in today. The Psalm layout is this: hear me, Lord; judge the situation justly; save me! The Psalmist begins by invoking the name of God to rescue him (doing so calls upon God's power). The author sees calling on God's might as a tactic of power against the might of his enemies. In defending the Psalmist, God would be delivering a fair verdict for legal justice.

Ruthless people are attacking the author; there are no mercy rulings here. These individuals have no concern for God and are out for blood. The Psalmist's last hope is God, who he names his helper. God has the final say over the author's life, and the Psalmist is so confident of His help that he believes that the God of justice will shift the outcome of the story. Instead of the Psalmist being put to an end, his enemies will come to their demise. Now, it is the Psalmist who is out for blood.

In thanks for his life, the Psalmist offers a sacrifice to the LORD, not out of obligation or law but out of gratitude. He believes he was delivered from impossible circumstances.

What Does This Imply?

There is power in the name of God. In calling out to God, one calls out for His might and deliverance. In calling on God, the Psalmist gives us an understanding of the reverence and trust he had in God's power against his enemies.

The Psalmist, fearing insurmountable judgement from his enemies, ironically jumps to offer his judgement for the strangers he speaks of too. The author describes the character of these persons, focusing on how they don't recognize God. Real justice may not prevail because of the strangers lack of character. The strangers may be geographical or simply people our author didn't know. In either case, the Psalmist laments that they don't know his innocence or character and seek to judge him wrongly, so they should be destroyed.

The author names God as helper and the One who must be on the Psalmist's side. If God is the Psalmist's helper, he can be confident that he is going to be fine! The Psalm concludes on a high note. In one fell swoop, we've moved from a man crying out for deliverance to a man thanking God for delivering him. The Psalmist proclaims, God has delivered me and gives me victory over my enemies!

In summary, the Psalmist begins on a note of worry but, upon self-examination, recovers himself, recognizing his victory by calling on the name of God.

How are We Invited to Respond?

It's hard to admit, but we don't control every aspect of our lives. In fact, we may find ourselves periodically in situations that feel helpless. When we face the psychological battle of hopelessness, this Psalm teaches us a few things.

- We may call on the name of God to remind us of His might against our enemies.

- We may be careful about taking on a 'mightier than thou' trap of superiority against those who seem against us. The Psalmist's actions are a demonstration of a man out for blood.

- In calling upon God, we may be filled with His strength, which surpasses our feelings and circumstances. As such, may we be reminded of God's faithfulness.

- We may respond to God's graciousness and His salvation through gratitude; it is a natural response to knowing and experiencing God's truth and might. The sinful woman's anointing of Jesus in the New Testament echoes this sentiment (see Luke 7:36–50). Because the woman received salvation, she engaged in acts of gratitude. So should we.

Questions for Reflection

1. Is there a situation that you face today that feels hopeless?

2. Are we willing to allow God to rescue us on His terms and not how we think things should go? Call on God's might to help you surrender your circumstances to Him today.

Day Twenty-Five: Psalm 55

What Does This Mean?

If you're reading this Psalm thinking, there's a lot going on here, you would be right. This Psalm is a composite of shorter laments.

The beginning of the Psalm meets an author at the end of his rope. He gives a roaring cry to God to hear him. The Psalmist's enemies roar, too, with threats and allegations. A kind of hunt is ensuing that breeds fear and desperation in our author. He wishes to escape his situation.

Political upheaval in the city creates further strife. Picture a city facing violence, looting, murder, and dishonest actions. But that's not all.

The deepest sorrow the Psalmist faces is the loss of someone who he considered a good friend. The identity of the friend is speculated (I would venture King Saul).

Our Psalmist jumps around again to call for the death of his enemies.

Are you ready? One more shift.

The author resolves to cast his cares on God; he is sure the LORD will hear him and rescue him. In addressing the betrayal of a close friend who has delivered false promises and empty words, the Psalmist will cast the burden to God and let Him handle his situation. God will surely not let the righteous fall.

What Does This Imply?

A composite Psalm makes it difficult to narrow down a singular problem to address. This Psalm has ninety-nine problems, and simplicity isn't one.

The Psalm seems to speak to one wound that reaches deeper into the soul than others—the betrayal of a friend. Having a betrayal piled on top of a city in chaos with enemies pursuing his life adds to the drama of the text.

To deal with his enemies, the Psalmist utters a wish to fly away from the city and have his enemies destroyed. In order to deal with a spirit crushed through betrayal, the Psalmist decides to call on God, casting his burdens on Him. Believing God and himself to be righteous, the Psalmist cannot conceive of a possibility that God would not rescue him.

How are We Invited to Respond?

When we are in anguish, how readily do we desire to escape and find rest from our circumstances? How eager are we to find a quiet corner of the world where we can be free from those who wound us? In my own life, I've come to find that the longer I distract myself from hard circumstances, the longer I am actually dealing with the problem. I can't emphasize enough that in lament, we don't need to put a timer on grief. We can't rush through our hurt to say we got to the other side. Grief won't be cheated. At the same time, we can't flee and avoid our problems.

Our Psalmist names three strategies for coping in his lament.

1. Escape his enemies
2. Destroy his enemies
3. Cast his burdens on God

The Psalm ends with the author processing through door number three, and I think we will benefit from walking the same path. We may throw, fling, and cast the circumstances of our lives onto God. The Psalmist appeals to God's duty to His people. God won't let the righteous drop because it's not in God's nature as the originator of righteousness to do so. Do you feel like doing some casting today?

Questions for Reflection

1. In times of distress, are you more prone to escape the situation, seek to destroy those who hurt you, or cast your burdens on God? Why do you think this is?

2. What do you seek to cast onto the LORD today?

Day Twenty-Six: Psalm 56

What Does This Mean?

Another day, another example of the havoc the Psalmist's enemies wreak on his spirit. Another day, another example of his swaying perspective between desperation and hope.

We don't know the exact enemy our author talks about, but we do know that the Psalmist is feeling the weight of pressure coming from enemy attacks. Our author writes with the poetic vigor of one who feels they are being hunted. The author's enemies have strength. They've got perseverance. Yet, our Psalmist asks, if I trust God, what's the worst human enemies can do to me? Calling on God, the Psalmist hopes that his trust serves as an offering whereby God would see fit to not allow his enemies to get away with their wickedness.

The Psalm takes a bit of a dramatic turn. Our author cries, God, You see me in my wrestling! You see how many tears I have cried; You've recorded how many!

A final shift occurs when the Psalmist returns to composed strength. He thinks, God is on my side. When called upon, my enemies will know and see God's power and will retreat as a result. The Psalmist is ready to worship as though victory over his enemies has already come. Surely, our author thinks, God will protect me, and so he responds with gratitude. The author hasn't been overlooked. God's taking out his enemies and counting his tears, making the Psalmist joyful and able to walk in light with God.

What Does This Imply?

The premise of the Psalmist's argument is God should avenge my enemies because of my trust in Him and because of my tears. A group of enemies should be taken out on the basis that they cause distress to the Psalmist to the point that he fears for his life.

The idea that God would count the tears of the Psalmist suggests that nothing, not even a tear, is so small that the LORD would not give attention to it. The author uses hyperbole to emphasize the nature of God.

As the Psalmist calls on God, his enemies would retreat because to call on the name of God is to invoke His might. Human might versus God's might? Even though the author has painted his enemies as strong, there's no contest. God wins every time.

In response to what the Psalmist believes is a sure-fire victory, he praises God with gratitude and joy. When our hearts are revived after our suffering, gratitude and joy arise.

How are We Invited to Respond?

"I praise God for what he has promised. I trust in God, so why should I be afraid? What can mere mortals do to me?" – Psalm 56:11

Repetition in Scripture is a little bit like ALL CAP MARKS FOR US TODAY. If something is repeated, early listeners of the text would be sure to pay attention. Today, we should notice how verses 4 and 11 repeat.

There is something within us that cannot be destroyed because of God's mercy and how He has created us. Today, we would call it a soul. As Jesus prepares his disciples for the mission field, he says, don't fear what can kill the body, but can't kill the soul; fear the One who can kill both (Matthew 10:28). The One who can do both? God. Only God has the power to defeat body, mind, and soul. No one else does.

We may find comfort in this thought when we are defeated by our circumstances. No one can take away our souls, our core being, because of God and His mercy. When we trust in God, particularly in hardship, we trust God to preserve the innermost part of ourselves. With our souls, and God's preservation of them, we may endure what comes our way.

Questions for Reflection

1. What is your understanding of the human soul?

2. How does the idea that, apart from God, your soul cannot be taken from you impact you today?

Day Twenty-Seven: Psalm 57

What Does This Mean?

Like Psalm 56, in Psalm 57, we find the Psalmist fearing for his life. Both Psalms begin with a call for mercy from God.

The author cries out to God, believing that God will continue His pattern of sustaining the Psalmist for a purpose (in rescuing him, God ensures His purpose for him will continue). Why does God do all of that? The Psalmist maintains that it is out of God's love for His faithful people.

The author continues painting a caricature of his enemies—they are predatory lions out for blood. He states that God would be exalted among his enemies because of his deliverance from his circumstances.

Verse 6 begins with fear as the Psalmist's enemies seek to trap him, and he is weary from the stress of his circumstances. His enemies wait for their prey (our author) to fall into their trap, but the Psalmist's tune shifts when he notes that the trap set for him by his enemies will not lead to his demise but theirs. The Psalmist praises God as a testimony to His love and faithfulness. The author's problems and despair have seemingly passed.

What Does This Imply?

As the Psalmist cries out for mercy, the reader may note his implicit belief that God will deliver him because God's nature is one that seeks to care for His hurting and suffering people. Of further note, the author turning to God for refuge is a regular practice according to the Hebrew verb tense used. As one of God's chosen people, God will protect the Psalmist.

The Psalmist also assumes that God will help him because God has always helped him accomplish the purposes of his life. What God sets out to accomplish as part of God's will will be accomplished. The author sees his life as one of purpose that cooperates with God's will. So, God will send His love and faithfulness to the Psalmist's rescue.

It is likely that the Psalmist's enemies are human, and the bestial language used is poetic. However, some scholars believe that the author speaks of real lions and references human enemies later in the Psalm.[9] Faced with deadly enemies in either case, the Psalmist makes an appeal—God, show Yourself and Your power! Deliver me! And when You do, may everyone see Your glory shine all over the earth!

The Psalmist's enemies seek to trap him, but in a prophetic vision, he sees that God will give him victory instead of his demise, and his enemies will fall into the same trap set for him. With the weight of a thousand pounds removed from his soul, the Psalmist envisions rejoicing as a witness to all that God has done.

How are We Invited to Respond?

The phrase, "Be exalted, O God, above the highest heavens! May your glory shine over all the earth" (Psalm 57:5) appears twice in this Psalm. Repetition marks something we should pay attention to in the Bible. The first time these words are uttered, the phrase appears as an argument for God to deliver the Psalmist. It's as if the Psalmist is saying, God, deliver me, because wow— what a compelling witness that will be to Your name! May Your name be exalted to the highest heavens because of the witness born of Your delivering me.

The second time the phrase appears, deliverance has likely been accomplished or has at least been as good as accomplished in the Psalmist's mind. This time the statement reflects the idea of a man who has been delivered, so God's name should be exalted.

In our lament, can we be so bold as to pray expectantly and with the hope of deliverance, "Be exalted, O God, above the highest heavens. May your glory shine over all the earth" (Psalm 57:11)? When we find ourselves at the height of another mountain top climbed, can we remember to proclaim, "Be exalted, O God, above the highest heavens. May your glory shine over all the earth" (Psalm 57:11)?

Questions for Reflection

1. In praying the phrase, "Be exalted, O God, above the highest heavens. May your glory shine over all the earth" (Psalm 57:11), are your words a prayer for hopeful deliverance or words of praise and thanks?

2. When we reflect on God's deliverance, we might think of deliverance on our terms. How might God be working to deliver us from our circumstances in unexpected ways?

Day Twenty-Eight: Psalm 59

What Does This Mean?

Our Psalm opens with four cries: rescue me, protect me, rescue me, and save me. David's enemies emerge at the request of King Saul, who wants the threat to his throne gone.

One can picture a group of warriors waiting to ambush David—an ambush that seeks to kill a man unfairly accused of trying to usurp the throne. In his innocence, the Psalmist begs God to see his circumstances and help. He wishes to see the warriors punished.

The Psalmist offers a description of his enemies; it's an unpleasant, fearsome picture. But they are no match for God and His ability to provide strength and safety. God's love will ensure God's intervention.

With victory on his mind, the Psalmist's thoughts turn dark. He doesn't want his enemies killed too quickly. The Psalmist thinks a quick death would be too easy. Instead, he would prefer that they experience the full consequences for their words, pride, curses, and lies. Then his enemies can be consumed by God's wrath. At their destruction, the world will know God.

Confident that his prayers will be answered, the Psalmist offers praise to God for God's power. God has shown up as refuge and demonstrated love for the innocent.

What Does This Imply?

The Psalmist's circumstances are, to put it plainly, *bad.* He's got no chance of living without God's help. The way he pleads his innocence appeals to a belief about God: God protects the innocent.

Unsurprisingly, the Psalmist doesn't speak favorably about his enemies. Surprisingly, we see just how much David wants his enemies to suffer God's wrath. (Remember, this is the guy who just got done telling God about his innocence.)

The Psalmist calls on God to reveal His power and might so that the world would know Him. The added benefit? David's enemies are no more.

At the end of the Psalm, we see a man utterly delighted at the thought of his enemies being brought down to shame and annihilation. David is so thrilled that it inspires him to worship. Such is the heart of a weary, unhealthy man.

How are We Invited to Respond?

As the Psalmist is describing his enemies, we may note a few contrasts between David and God.

- The Psalmist fears for his life, while God laughs and scoffs at hostile nations.
- The Psalmist sees fierce enemies, but God triumphs over people.

Where humans fear their circumstances, God oversees the whole of creation.

No matter your circumstances, when we face obstacles that seem insurmountable, we can call upon God for rescue. God cares for the innocent. God cares for those in situations so dangerous it seems that all hope is lost. God cares for those overwhelmed by their life circumstances, and those who aren't sure how to make it through to the next day.

The Psalmist offers a prayer that we can pray today: God, rescue me. God, protect me. God, rescue me. God, save me.

While I don't recommend telling God how to punish those who contribute to your difficult circumstances, I do invite us to envision the day when we can offer God praise because God has helped us overcome the situation that felt like all the odds were stacked against us.

Questions for Reflection

1. What do you imagine God's protection looks like? If you are uncertain or desire wisdom in this, go to Him in prayer and ask God what His protection for your life looks like. Listen.

2. Pray for yourself or over a loved one: "God, rescue (name). God, protect (name). God, rescue (name). God, save (name). Amen."

Day Twenty-Nine: Psalm 61

What Does This Mean?

A man with a tired, feeble heart cries out to God. Our author is likely displaced from home. He may be displaced spiritually because of how low he feels, displaced physically from Jerusalem, or perhaps a bit of both. With his sense of security lost and feeling physically weak, the Psalmist prays for a haven in God's presence. There, his enemies cannot reach him.

The Psalmist calls on God to be faithful as a reminder that God has a covenant to uphold. Shifting from lament to a word of hope, our author muses, You have heard me, God. You have sheltered me and let me dwell with You. The Psalmist is pleased to have received such an honor as to experience God's presence. Surely, there is no sweeter place to exist.

The Psalm shifts at verse 6 with the author requesting more years of life for the king and to let the king rule in God's presence. Further, he asks that God protect the king in his reign.

In conclusion, the Psalmist offers that because God demonstrated His faithfulness in providing protection and security, He will be praised, and the author will be faithful to his vows.

What Does This Imply?

Our author is lonely and afraid. Feeling isolated from a sense of home, he cries out to God for comfort. He has lost heart and vigor for life, and we witness a kind of physical and spiritual depletion within him.

The Psalmist asks for God's leading, suggesting that he might be feeling lost as well. God leading him to a place of safety ensures he finds a sense of hope and direction again. God's shelter provides the safety and security that the Psalmist so desperately seeks.

When we approach the shift in focus from himself to that of the king, we may wonder why our Psalmist would plead for the king's safety and well-being. Likely, the author would benefit in some way with his king in power, or at least, he believes his life would be more favorable with the king. We might interpret the topic of king to mean throne, specifically the throne of Israel. If Israel's throne is established and safely secured, our Psalmist will breathe a sigh of relief and give thanks.

Throughout the Psalm the idea of God's covenants to Israel could be on the author's mind as he calls God to be faithful in rescuing him. Should God keep His side of the bargain, this man will stay faithful to his vows (imperfectly, as Israel's history demonstrates).

How are We Invited to Respond?

Can you think of a single person in your life who hasn't had some kind of experience with loneliness? Loneliness is the sense of otherness when one struggles to connect with community for a variety of reasons. Loneliness can happen in times of growth and transition, as the result of loss, or might even feel like the norm for some people.

When the Psalmist is lonely, he calls out to God as his lifeline. In God, he finds safety, security, and companionship.

It is in God's presence where we might find reprieve from our own loneliness and insecurity. If you're a college student adjusting to being on your own for the first time, let God be your refuge. If you're an elderly person who longs for the company of friends who have gone on to glory, let God be your shelter. If you're a single person seeking to carve out your place in the world, let God be your rock. For the newly empty nesters, the mom or dad navigating the world of parenting, and everyone in between, God can be our sanity.

How might we seek God's presence?

- We make time for what matters. Make time today for stillness in a space with little to no distractions. Invite God's presence into your space.
- We pour the contents of our thoughts out to God.
- We stop, listen, and learn what God might have to say to us.

Questions for Reflection

1. What are your experiences with loneliness?

2. How does God meet us in loneliness?

Day Thirty: Psalm 64

What Does This Mean?

We find ourselves reading a unique Psalm today—one chock full of political charge. The Psalmist finds himself in the thick of a plot for his life. His enemies scheme behind his back, making him the target of a hunt. The author asks God to protect the righteous and upright in heart, marking this not only as a Psalm for an individual but for corporate loyalists to the throne.

Our Psalm begins with a prayer for protection and courage to not be overwhelmed by fear, before the author moves into a description of his enemies, counting how they use their words against the righteous. He questions the contents of their minds and hearts.

The Psalm shifts to a vision of God shooting down the author's enemies (note the poetic contrast between enemy arrows and God's arrows). But it is the words of the Psalmist's enemies that will be the final nail in their coffin. A (metaphorical) veil will be removed, and people will see them for who they are and recognize God's might.

The Psalm concludes with a call to let the righteous rejoice! Those who do the right thing, let them praise God.

What Does This Imply?

At the forefront of the Psalmist's mind is the assumption that he and the godly (described as those who are righteous and upright in heart) have the moral high ground in the scenario at hand.

The Psalmist asks for protection against opposition. He prays for courage to stand in the face of political insult because the minds and hearts of his enemies are cunning. Since his enemies stand opposed to the righteous, the Psalmist believes that God will use the same weapon (arrows) intended to harm the godly against the wicked. The words of the enemy will be the enemies' ultimate downfall. Their words and beliefs trust in false things. The Psalmist's words show trust in God. Upon the enemies' destruction, the people will see things as they really are, and the godly will rejoice and praise God.

How are We Invited to Respond?

It is at least implicitly, if not explicitly, stated that the Psalmist's enemies have built their lives on empty promises, powers, and hopes. When this happens, a time will appear when what has always been empty is revealed to be empty.

When we place our aspirations, hopes, words, or lives into the hands of anything less than God, we are sure to turn up empty ourselves. But when our words, deeds, and lives demonstrate a foundation built from God's goodness, we are a witness to His character. Our witness to God's truth and goodness also occurs when we seek to do what is right. Those who seek to do what is right have the privilege of standing back in awe of His work in this world and offering Him praise.

To be sure, it is not my advice to take this Psalm literally and wish for the demise of our enemies (political or otherwise). Instead, we should pray for our enemies (see Matthew 5:44–45), continue to do the next right thing, and let God sort out the rest.

The Psalmist hopes God will protect him from enemy words and help him face those words and blows with courage. May we do the same.

Questions for Reflection

1. Take a moment to think about the top three things that you invest time in each week. Do these investments suggest a life built on empty promises or a life built on God?

2. What does it look like to face with courage those who oppose us?

Day Thirty-One: Psalm 70

What Does This Mean?

Historically, this Psalm has been used during memorial offerings where sacrifices were made in the hope that God would look favorably on a person.[10]

The Psalmist asks God to come to his rescue quickly. The author's life is in danger, but scholars generally believe that the urgency of this Psalm is lower than that of others.[11] The Psalmist wishes to see those who delight in his trouble disgraced. For those who seek to destroy him, he wants them to be humiliated. On the other hand, he hopes that those who search for God would have joy and offer praise to the Lord.

The Psalmist describes himself as poor and needy (perhaps as part of a spiritual, rather than a physical, deficit). He invokes God as helper and savior to rescue him quickly from his circumstances.

What Does This Imply?

Have you ever thought about God's choice of timing? Psalm 70 invites us to consider when God will act on the author's behalf. The Psalmist asks a question about God's moral behavior. When the author begs for God to deliver him quickly and make his enemies pay for their actions, we might begin to see his idea of what a good and moral God would, and perhaps should, do in his situation. A good and moral God would surely care about the author's circumstances and be quick to deliver him from.

How are We Invited to Respond?

If you've ever been in a situation where your circumstances have felt desperate or where you've been hanging on by a thread, you understand actively seeking to get out of that situation as quickly as possible. Our Psalmist wants this for himself. But it might be wise to take this Psalm as a warning. We must be wary of setting a timetable for God. Since we are so wrapped up in time, it can be difficult to imagine a God who exists beyond the realm of time.

If we create a timetable for God to work in, we risk a few things:

- Disappointment: If we set boundaries for God, it doesn't mean He will limit Himself to those same boundaries. We may find ourselves disappointed in a god we've created and tried to coerce.
- Missed development: If we use a timetable to close ourselves off to God's work, we may miss out on developing critical faith muscles. Or we may find ourselves developing muscles for trust in ourselves. If God does not answer our timetable, we may take it upon ourselves to act as we see morally fit, missing a critical

opportunity for development in our faith. But if we extend our faith to say, God, rescue me in Your time, we may find ourselves amazed by what He will do.

We should not fear asking God for His help. He delights in our trust and our hope in Him to deliver us. But we should seek to surrender our timetable for rescue because in doing so, we extend trust to God. We trust that He is a moral, trustworthy God, working with the big picture in mind—a redeemed and restored world.

If you find yourself seeking rescue from the world's harsh realities, take heart. God is working. God is restoring. God is healing. And He is doing so in ways we can't imagine.

Questions for Reflection

1. If God is working to create a restored and redeemed world, how does that shape how we view our current circumstances?

2. What does surrender to God's timing look like in your life today?

Day Thirty-Two: Psalm 71

What Does This Mean?

Today, we find our Psalmist writing from the perspective of an older man. The author calls on God for rescue and the preservation of his dignity. His old age has not dissuaded enemies but given them opportunities to exploit physical weakness.

The Psalmist reflects on his life and how through it, God acted as his rock. His life is a witness to God's faithfulness, so he asks that in his old age, God would deliver him again as his enemies seek to take advantage of his situation.

Our author's urgency for deliverance increases. He asks God to disgrace his enemies in the community (a fate worse than death in the culture). Suddenly, the Psalm shifts to an attitude of hope—he believes his deliverance is at hand, and he will praise God for such relief.

The Psalmist reflects on how he called upon God's help from his youth and was answered. He asks again that in his old age, God would renew his spirits. His life has been a series of hardships, but the Lord has renewed him each time. The Psalmist trusts God to restore him presently.

The Psalm concludes with the author's deliverance; he has escaped his plotting enemies, and they have received shame and humiliation as punishment for their actions.

What Does This Imply?

As the Psalmist calls out to God, consider the physical limitations that come with age, making our author vulnerable to attack. There is also a sense of the Psalmist's loneliness as he seeks God's refuge. He fears he is not strong enough to protect himself from his enemies. As an elderly person seeks to be treated with honor and dignity, he seeks not to be disgraced.

Since his birth, God has shown His faithfulness to the Psalmist. In asking God to rescue him, even in his old age, the author appeals to God that his life may be a continuing witness to His power. By intervening, God dispels the enemies' claim that He has abandoned the author.

As the Psalm moves towards a hopeful note, experience reminds the Psalmist of God's good nature and character. God has been his hope all his life, creating a pattern: God showed up, and the Psalmist praised Him.

After counting life's joys and hardships, the Psalmist praises God once again. Devotion to faith in God has renewed his spirits. What was inescapable, God has helped him escape.

How are We Invited to Respond?

Aging is a universal human experience. From the moment we are born, we begin the aging process. It is interesting to consider the fear our culture associates with aging. We buy products, eat special diets, and do anything we can think of to stave off the effects of age or at least look a little younger.

Perhaps our fear of aging comes from the value we place on productivity. The aging process slows our ability to contribute in a way that culture deems beneficial. I wonder if there is room in our minds to expand what we consider to be of value.

If you've ever been in a nursing home or live in one yourself, you may know how many unique stories and experiences exist within such a place. People gifted with a wealth of knowledge and insight live together but often go unheard. Many people in a nursing home may find themselves lonely, longing for their spouses or friends who have passed away.

One woman who I visit in my travels as a pastor remains as pleasant as ever. I've never known someone so verbal, so repetitive in her praise to God. In each story that she tells, she reflects on where she considers God to have been a part of it. She doesn't gloss over the hard things in her life, but she faces them with dignity, grace, and perspective.

We forget that age offers something that youth can't give: perspective. Time to think. Time to reflect. Can you remember the last time you had a down moment and used that moment to consider God's faithfulness?

If we are to age with the grace and dignity of our Psalmist, we require the perspective to do so. Today seems like a great time to consider God's faithfulness in carrying you through the days of your life, no matter how long or short.

Questions for Reflection

1. What does it mean to be faithful?

2. Consider what your testimony of God's faithfulness would look like as of today. If you have not done so already, write your story down or make additions to the last time you reflected on this thought.

Day Thirty-Three: Psalm 77

What Does This Mean?

We can't pinpoint an exact reason for the anguish that the Psalmist brings to his writing, but we do know that he suffers. He begins calling out to God in unfiltered, unabandoned grief.

The Psalmist has searched for God's presence seemingly to no avail. He feels that God's mercy has run out, and he is so exhausted and overwhelmed that he doesn't know what to pray anymore. He pines after the days when he experienced great joy.

The author explores questions related to a sense of abandonment from the Lord. He demands in his grief, has God changed? The God who he knew to be compassionate, the God who he knew rescued, seems to be nowhere. Something is not matching up between the God he knew in his past and the God he knows now.

By examining God's work in human history, the Psalmist reconciles the emotional and logical nature of his situation, and his perspective changes to a hymn of praise. There is no God like his God. He is the God of miracles and wonders, the God of redemption and strength, and the God of deliverance.

What Does This Imply?

This Psalm offers us insight into the conflicts of the mind and heart of a person who works through and processes deep sorrow in the context of faith. Our Psalmist wrestles with doubt, as he seeks to make sense of God within his difficult circumstances. Interestingly, his questions do not produce faithlessness; instead, they lead him to a realization of who God is.

The Psalmist questions what he knows about God and how God responds to his situation (or rather, seemingly doesn't respond). He wonders, has God changed? Perhaps it is humanity's ability to comprehend the truth of who God is that shifts and morphs. The author realizes upon introspection that he isn't finding the answers he seeks, so he turns straight to the source of his questions—he considers God Himself. The author switches from subjective musings about the pain in his life and God's involvement in it to objective thoughts on who God is, as revealed in God's work in human history.

Upon remembering the stories and accounts of God's faithfulness, the Psalmist grows in confidence in his knowledge of and relationship to God. The Psalmist directly references three stories in Scripture: Jacob, Joseph, and the Exodus narrative. One could make a case that the creation of the world is implicitly interweaved into the poem, too. These histories produce confidence in God's sovereignty.

How are We Invited to Respond?

When we process significant grief, loss, or suffering, we may find ourselves asking the same questions our Psalmist did in verses 7–9:

- "Has the Lord rejected me forever?"
- "Will he never again be kind to me?"
- "Is his unfailing love gone forever?"
- "Have his promises permanently failed?"
- "Has God forgotten to be gracious?"
- "Has he slammed the door on his compassion?"

In our lament, we may experience a range and depth of emotions we didn't know we could feel in such a short amount of time.

Some would criticize doubt as a sign of disobedience or sin. To be clear, doubt can lead to disobedience, but it can also lead to genuine, honest clarity and the understanding of a good and holy God. The layout of Psalm 77 shares a man processing difficult circumstances mentally and emotionally. He found it difficult to truly see God through a cloud of emotions, but when he stepped back and reflected on God's acts in human history, he could see clearly the God he had spent a lifetime praising.

Our own introspection in lament may act as a starting point of reflection, but if we are to know and experience God in hard circumstances, recounting His work in human history is a means of reconciling our situation with our thoughts and emotions and, most importantly, enabling a stronger understanding of God.

Questions for Reflection

1. Read three Bible stories:

    - Jacob's Story: Genesis 25:19–34; 27:1–38; 28:10–22
    - Joseph's Story: Genesis 37; 42:6–7; 45:1–11
    - The Exodus Narrative: Exodus 14

1. How do you see God's faithfulness to His people in these stories?

1. How do these stories speak to your current circumstances?

Day Thirty-Four:
Psalm 86

What Does This Mean?

The exact case of distress for our Psalmist is once again unknown; however, we might consider a few possibilities, such as ruthless enemies or the author's sin (though this idea is debated by scholars based on their interpretation of the text).[12] Either way, the Psalmist seems to experience a combination of internal and external stressors. This Psalm jumps around a bit. We may find ourselves reading what feels like a conclusion to the work when suddenly, the Psalmist delves back into his problems, before making his final point.

The Psalmist opens by asking, Hear my prayer for preservation because I trust in You, God. He is helpless in the face of his affliction.

The author continues, pleading with God to bring him mercy and give his soul joy. He makes the case that God is good and forgiving, and as such, He should help the Psalmist. God is good, so

He helps those in need. The Psalmist notes more characteristics of God: there is no other like God; God is the performer of miracles; God is worthy to be praised.

To gain greater understanding and clarity, the Psalmist asks God to teach him His truth and faithfulness. Our author wants his heart to look like God's heart and turns to reflect on God's help in previous times of deep despair.

It seems the Psalmist faces dangerous enemies, yet his confidence in God to show mercy and rescue him is evident. The Psalm concludes with a final ask: send a demonstration of grace to me that will help and comfort me while shaming my enemies.

What Does This Imply?

One might view this prayer as a kind of persuasive essay to God to intervene on behalf of our Psalmist, interpreting this passage as the Psalmist arguing in favor of his holiness—his circumstances aren't a result of his own sin, and therefore, he makes the perfect candidate for a good God to help him.

One could also interpret the Psalm as arguing that the Psalmist has sinned and because of this, discusses God's mercy and ability to forgive.

The prayer delves into God's character as capable of mighty acts. We might imagine our Psalmist considering God's history in his life and realizing his own circumstances would be easy for God to handle.

The Psalmist goes on to consider that by knowing God's truth and being faithful to it, he can face whatever comes his way. He reflects that God's presence with him has already offered rescue from an earlier season of deep despair.

The author's enemies are a ruthless bunch, but their violence is no match for God's mercy. The Psalmist's prayer will be answered with grace to help him through his circumstances.

How are We Invited to Respond?

I like independence. I like freedom. Don't you?

Autonomy is something we value. We like making our own choices and feeling like we are in control of our lives. But what happens when life hits us with events that are out of our control? Such events make it difficult for us to know how to move forward; they might even feel impossible to tackle on our own.

Freedom is a gift given to us by God, through Jesus. We are free from oppression and sin, we are free from bonds and death, and we are invited to use the freedom that we have been given and offer it back to God in service.

This Psalm offers a prayer with a similar idea: help my mind be in line with Yours. In taking our freedom and turning our thought life to the mind of God, we may live truthfully and faithfully, thanks to the instruction of our faithful teacher. We live in such a way that honors God's love for us. We receive wisdom to walk well in our lives and face the pitfalls of life in healthy ways.

If we find ourselves in a position of lament uncertain of what to do next, whether the cause is a result of our poor choices or not, we might take a step of faithfulness and ask God how we might go on living well. It isn't a question of whether God will help us learn His truth but of whether we will pursue His truth in the first place.

Questions for Reflection

1. How do you imagine one gets to know the heart of God?

2. How does God invite you to live in alignment with Him today?

Day Thirty-Five: Psalm 89

What Does This Mean?

This Psalm shows someone calling out to God on behalf of their king. Moving in parts, this work begins by declaring God's faithfulness to His promises. The Psalm moves into a joyful examination of God's power as evidenced in creation. There is no one like God; He rules over the seas, defeats any other god's "competition," created north and south, demonstrates moral sovereignty, and is merciful. Those who know God walk in joy, for they recognize their strength and defense.

Verse 19 echoes the prophet Nathan's words to King David (2 Samuel 7:4–17), which articulates God's promises. David received special favor from the Lord, as well as an enduring lineage. Should David's line be disobedient, consequences would arise, but God's promises would not be revoked. David's descendants would endure.

Our lament begins at verse 38; the king has been cast off, and the author dances around the idea of God remembering His covenant to the Davidic line. The king's neighbors reproach him, his enemies mock him, and he exists in shame. How long, our author asks, must the king suffer? Where is Your mercy and kindness, God?

The Psalm ends with a call: remember Your people, God (the king's actions impact more than just the king). Blessed be Your name, Amen.

What Does This Imply?

Life is full of navigating relationships, and this Psalm addresses God's existence and the nature of God in relationship to Israel and Israel's king. The angels themselves recognize God's wonders as evidence of His majesty. Listing off His cosmic resume, the Psalmist appeals to His mighty hand. To call God a shield of Israel was to affirm His existence.

In all of creation, God chose man (and specifically speaks of King David) as an agent for God's will to be actualized on earth. God engages with David (and his lineage) in a covenant. David would be faithful to God, and God faithful to David. David's moral actions solidified the promise of a healthy lineage and power. And even if he or his lineage disobeyed God, He would still be faithful in His purposes for humanity. God's side of the covenant was irrevocable. The Psalmist recalls the Davidic covenant, asking God to remember His promises.

Moving into a mood of lament, the Psalmist questions the security of the line of David because of human error. We may recognize that David's line has failed morally. The consequences of sin are present in the king's suffering. The crown is in shame, and enemies plunder what isn't theirs and laugh at Israel's misfortune. The king is rapidly aging due to the stressors in his life.

It is important to note that the Psalmist is not accusing God of causing any kind of fault within the king. The author is appealing to God's compassion to change Israel's circumstances because of the covenant made.

How are We Invited to Respond?

This is a prayer written on behalf of another whose actions have impacted the whole of Israel. This writer mourns the damage and suffering around him and asks God to remember His covenant and offer mercy and compassion.

This Psalm reflects care and compassion in two forms:

1. For the individual who has been kicked down by their actions in a way that they may never have imagined.

2. For the community of those who hurt alongside the hurting person.

We may know people who have made choices that harm them and their community. If you grieve for a friend, family member, co-worker, etc. who hurts because they are feeling the weight and shame of moral failings, here's how you might offer them care:

1. Pray for them to remember (or discover) God's character, even in their pain.

2. Pray for their hearts to know God's great compassion.

3. Pray for them to confess their moral failing and need for a Savior.

4. Pray for them to receive God's mercy and be changed by His love.

Questions for Reflection

1. Is there someone in your life who is hurting because of past or current moral failings? Pray for them.

2. What does this Psalm tell us about the value of community in lament?

Day Thirty-Six: Psalm 102

What Does This Mean?

If you've read Psalm 102 and think that it's all over the place, you wouldn't be wrong!

If you've experienced any kind of short or long-term illness, you may understand the cry of the Psalmist when he calls out, help, God! I'm sick! He has a painful illness that leaves him without appetite and reduces him to skin and bones.

On top of physical ailment, the Psalmist is lonely and mocked by his enemies. The author assumes that the circumstances he faces are a result of his personal actions that have, apparently, brought on God's wrath. He believes being outside of God's favor is the reason that he withers away to nothing.

A shift takes place at verse 12, however. Hope is born out of a state of despair. The Psalmist hopes in a future for Jerusalem, where the city will be rebuilt, and God's glory will shine on the destitute and hurting. God's rebuilding Jerusalem reminds the author of God's faithfulness. God, not man, will be known (for generations) as the One who looked upon the cry of those unjustly condemned and set them free. The response of the people will be praise and adoration. God's name will be known for all days.

A final transition takes place at verse 23. We return to a similar note to the beginning of our Psalm. The Psalmist asks God to restore him to his youth so that his time on earth would not be cut short. He reflects on a note of hope that was missing earlier in the lament: God created the earth, and while the earth is temporary, God and His character remain the same forever. As such, His people may rest in the security of God's trustworthiness.

What Does This Imply?

The contents of the Psalm deal with physical, mental, and spiritual issues. It takes the reality and trustworthiness of God seriously.

The Psalmist, likely dealing with a stomach issue or fever that his doctors and medicine are not yet equipped to handle, asks God for deliverance. When a person is ill, the reality of other aspects of life can become cloudy. It becomes easier for a person to experience spiritual depletion. The Psalmist implies that his illness is the consequence of his own actions. As such, the historic church initially used this as a Psalm of penitence (a work used to express repentance). It is entirely true that our actions and choices may breed illness. As such, we should take responsibility for our actions and receive the mercy and freedom granted by God's grace. But it is also important not to make a blanket statement about illness out of this Psalm. Not all sicknesses are directly caused by one's choices. Illness, as we know, exists because of a broken world. We would do well to shepherd our words thoughtfully when speaking to someone with an illness, both to help them tend to their soul's well-being and to not promote unnecessary shame or guilt.

The Psalmist continues with a description of loneliness. He describes himself as a bird outside of its natural environment. Loneliness strikes deeply because we believe others are out in the world living while we are surviving. The Psalmist's situation is worsened by those who mock him.

A sort of hymn interrupts the Psalmist's outpouring of pain (perhaps we are dealing with more than one author of this poem). The poet reflects on God's sovereignty and faithfulness, namely through the vision of Jerusalem restored for the sake of rescuing God's people. God rebuilds places and people who have experienced destruction at their own hands to show that He is a God of mercy. In God rescuing innocent prisoners, we see a God of justice.

The Psalmist lands on the idea that God is trustworthy because God is the same God throughout history. God's deeds and character are sure—we know the final story where God's people are restored. Because of who God is, God's people can take security in uncertain circumstances.

How are We Invited to Respond?

"But you are always the same; you will live forever. The children of your people will live in security." – Psalm 102:27–28

When we encounter situations where we feel isolated because of our circumstances, it's easy to spiral down a road of despair. Illness of the physical and mental variety provides ample opportunity for such isolation. Where is the hope for those who suffer? This Psalm relays that hope is found in God's trustworthy nature. Some of us, for known and unknown reasons, will receive healing for wounds and illness. For others, for reasons known and unknown, full healing will not come in this lifetime. We can trust God to be a God of mercy and compassion because of the vision of restoration He has for creation. You and I probably don't have a clue about God's timing, but because God is the same (and has demonstrated His trustworthiness throughout history), our security (and the security of generations) can be trusted.

Questions for Reflection

1. What is our responsibility in promoting a restored world?

2. Can I trust God to restore the uncertain, painful moments I have in my life?

Day Thirty-Seven: Psalm 120

What Does This Mean?

The Psalm begins with a recollection of a time when God answered the Psalmist's prayer. In reflection, he cries out again to the God who hears our cries and involves Himself in our lives. Specifically, our author seeks reprieve from lying tongues that perpetuate falsehoods.

The Psalmist wonders, what will God do with those with deceptive tongues? We might take this as a rhetorical question. The deceptive tongue will meet its end and painfully so.

Delving further into his suffering, our Psalmist explains that he exists in a land surrounded by those he considers barbaric because of their war-like speech. While he has tried to promote peace, everyone around him prefers to speak words that produce strife and war.

What Does This Imply?

The Psalmist remembering God's deliverance in his life reminds us that there are circumstances beyond our control when we can rely on God to do what we cannot. The Psalmist cries out to God because he knows that He can address this problem better than humans.

In our author's cry for deliverance against the deception of the human tongue, we see the power of such a tiny organ. We may note the personal wounds we've received at the hands of another's tongue. We may seek to be conscious of the use of our own weaponry.

The Psalmist uses interesting language around the punishment of those with deceptive tongues. He starts with a rhetorical question: what will God do to the deceiving tongue? Our author knows the answer or at least is confident in his own imaginings of what God will do. Rather than stating what he believes will happen to deceivers, he inserts God into the equation. It may be that the Psalmist felt that directly inserting his ideas for deceivers' punishment overstepped the judgement that belonged only to God. If so, it is interesting then that the Psalmist lists some suggestions for what would happen to the deceivers! We like to speculate on the demise of others, but do we see the judgement in our hearts as perpetuating a problem that is made known through our own speech? In any case, the fate of the deceiving tongue is grim.

Whether our author goes on to describe geographic coordinates for his living situation or uses them as a metaphor to communicate the kind of people he exists among—barbarians—note that our Psalmist seeks to create peace. "Blessed are the peacemakers, for they will be called children of God" (Matthew 5:9 NIV). It is through prayer and the cry of those who seek to pursue and perpetuate peace that our God has mercy on us and gives the gift of the Prince of Peace.

How are We Invited to Respond?

Big things come from a tiny organ—the tongue. Scripture testifies that the tongue can build or destroy. The words that we speak reveal what is in our hearts. Things like war. Things like peace.

The tongue can worship or curse. The tongue can be used for good or evil, and in a fallen world, evil still manages to be present, tearing down and hurting others. A hypocritical tongue is a natural default position, marked by bitter envy and selfish ambition. The tongue allows us to see the tension of living in a world awaiting redemption. Believers ought to always be growing more consistent in their speech.

We must know the source of the tongue's redemption. Redeemed speech comes from godly wisdom being imparted to us to know how we might use our words and promote peace. Worldly wisdom will lead to a tongue infused with bitterness that will show itself through bragging and denying the truth. Godly wisdom will lead to pure and peaceable speech.

It is in conversation with God, recognizing our reliance on Him for the wisdom to know the state of our hearts and speech, that we begin the first steps to perpetuating peace on earth.

Questions for Reflection

1. What does your tongue reveal about your heart today?

2. What wisdom would you seek from God to know how to perpetuate peace on earth?

Day Thirty-Eight: Psalm 139

What Does This Mean?

Have you ever taken some time to reflect on God's presence in your life? (Hint: if you've read this far, your answer is yes!) Our Psalmist writes in awe of God's omniscience (knowledge) and omnipresence (presence) based on the reflections of his life experiences. God knows the Psalmist and knows the actions and words that spring from his heart—even before he does or says them! God's presence is active and everywhere, ready to guide the Psalmist on a path of blessing. Even darkness cannot hide him from God. God's presence and power is sovereign.

The poem expands on how God formed the Psalmist into being, right down to his kidneys (the culture thought that this was the center of emotion). God formed the heart and the body. He saw the author as an embryo and recorded his life in a book where the moments were purposed before he was born.

God's thoughts about the Psalmist are valued and esteemed. He is humbled that God would think so much about him.

The Psalmist goes on, saying, if only God would destroy the wicked! He places himself as a foe to the wicked because of their disregard for God. The author wonders, should I hate those opposed to God? He decides, yes, he will completely hate those who are resistant to God.

In conclusion, the Psalmist ends his prayer saying, search me, God, and know my heart, thoughts, and what I care about. See if there is anything in my heart that will bring a life of pain. Lead me into life that yields what God has declared to be good and right.

What Does This Imply?

In God's ability to examine our hearts and know us, we encounter God's knowledge of ourselves to a level and degree that no one else has had or will have for us. Such intimate knowledge is beyond what we may know even about ourselves. God's knowledge extends beyond time and place.

So often, we might walk through this world feeling misunderstood, but God knows, really knows, the whole picture of who we are. The good, the bad, the pretty, the ugly—He knows it.

God's presence is everywhere, and God is sovereign over all places—even the place of death. Try as we might, we cannot hide ourselves from the His presence.

God not only knows us and is present with us, but He also creates us with purpose. He formed our hearts and bodies together (the Psalm isn't a scientific explanation but a poetic one). Such formation occurs with a purpose. God loves us. He delights in us. He calls us precious and considers our well-being.

Verse 19 takes a turn with talk of enemies, aka, those who blaspheme God's very existence. The author decides to hate the enemies of God for himself. We may wonder, is this a godly standard or a human venting frustration? Jesus addresses this idea clearly, "You have heard that it was said, 'Love your neighbor and hate your enemy.' But I tell you, love your enemies and pray for those who persecute you, that you may be children of your Father in heaven" (Matthew 5:43–45a NIV).

The Psalm ends with the prayer that God would search the author's heart and find evil within. From there, he invites God to root out what is wicked so that he may pursue what is right, leading to life everlasting. We cannot root evil out on our own. Through God's help, we become good.

How are We Invited to Respond?

When people read through Psalm 139, questions of predestination arise. Predestination is the idea that the steps of our lives are already formed and accounted for by God. Predestination in the Wesleyan tradition is described as conditional; God would elect all persons to be saved, but not everyone chooses to cooperate with their destiny. God remains all powerful in this situation because He restrains His own power for the sake of humanity's free will to choose or withdraw from Him.

But when we read of God forming us and counting our days, we may feel that we have little choice in our lives. Do we ever get to make a choice for ourselves?

Context is important in any Scriptural reading, so we need to consider the genre that we are reading today: poetry. God forming us and counting our days is used to illustrate His involvement and presence in our lives. It does not mean that you and I don't have a choice in how our lives play out.

Our hearts, gifts, minds, and bodies are formed in the womb. And yet, the use of these assets is shaped by our faith (or lack thereof). As human beings, we wrestle between seeking intimacy and seeking space from our Creator. God's presence with us means that we have a guide who is willing and able to show us how we might use our lives in what He has predetermined to be good and right. We may also choose to shy away from our Creator and use our gifts and bodies for personal gain.

In God forming our bodies and His presence with us, choice is not nullified. We must choose to develop our gifts and graces for His glory and the world's good. God knows us before we know ourselves because He is not restricted by the limits of time as we are. God has a purpose for our lives before we understand what purpose is. It may be comforting to think we are meant to become X, Y, or Z, but the greatest calling God offers, before any name, title, or position, is simply to be His child. As such, a sense of purpose becomes transformed from a restrictive formula to a relational connection.

The believer can choose to fulfill the purpose they are created for—to be a child of God. The believer can choose to have faith and to be obedient to God to become the person He has created them to be in full.

Who does the Psalmist call wicked in this poem? Those who disregard God as God. This is a choice.

In suffering and hardship, we may allow our hearts to be withdrawn in our lament. Or we may choose to continue in our purpose as a child of God, guided by a God who would help us walk into everlasting life.

Questions for Reflection

1. Is your heart drawn toward God or withdrawn from God?

2. Take some time to reflect on where you've seen God's presence in your life recently.

Day Thirty-Nine: Psalm 141

What Does This Mean?

Urgent. Passionate. Intense. Is it any wonder that a young person wrote this Psalm? During an evening worship service where a sacrifice is taking place, the Psalmist seeks God's ear for help against temptations brought on by the wicked. He doesn't want to seek after what the wicked are seeking; he wants to guard his speech and purify his heart.

But.

Temptation exists for our young author because the wicked seem to be encountering a level of prosperity he doesn't have. He doesn't *want* to do wicked things to gain prosperity. He doesn't *want* to be in company with them at their feasts, but our Psalmist may be experiencing a level of suffering for pursuing what is good and right.

The Psalmist cries, let me be punished by the godly—such punishment is better than to be anointed with oil from the wicked at their feasts. Why? Because the oil is temporary prosperity. The fate of the wicked is to end up in the land of the dead (Sheol).

The Psalm concludes with resolution: God, keep me in line! I'm looking to You for help! Don't let the wicked and their traps kill me. Keep me away from the traps of the wicked and let them receive the demise they set for me. But let me escape, God!

What Does This Imply?

Psalm 141 reads like the writings of a vulnerable human being. In the poem, there is fear, intensity, sincerity, imperfection, and honesty.

We may assume our author is young because when he seeks correction, he likely seeks it from older elders in the community. In this poem, a young man wrestles between following his instincts regarding the world and instincts involving God. Our author seeks to be unburdened from the struggle of his life, whether to give in to the temptation of the wicked with their seeming prosperity or flee from temptation and accept correction.

Part of the Psalmist's struggle involves controlling his speech. He decides that receiving correction from elders would be better medicine for his soul than to feast with and be anointed by the wicked. The author has some level of foresight to recognize that their feasting and anointing is temporary prosperity. Eternally, the wicked are destined for a wicked ending.

The Psalmist decides to turn his attention to God so that he may live and be guided through the traps set for him by the wicked. We see him conclude with a common request of the time: let my enemies fall into the trap that they have set for me. But let me go free! In essence, our Psalmist wants to see the wicked get what they deserve. This is a part of the prayer we may not want to absorb into our own lives. In Christ's measure, there is no longer an eye for an eye standard. All have fallen short of God's glory (Romans 3:23).

How are We Invited to Respond?

"Let the godly strike me! It will be a kindness!" – Psalm 141:5a

If given the choice, I would avoid pain like the plague. Maybe you would, too. Our Psalmist reads a little like a certifiable nutcase for signing up to receive a strike as a kindness. However, if we investigate the text a bit more, the striking has less to do with physical contact and more to do with verbal correction that acts like medicine to the soul. This strike is meant to restore our author to wholeness.

When we lament, our judgement of what is right and wrong can become cloudy. We need good, godly mentors around us that can help us make wise decisions at crucial (or regular) moments. To receive correction for our misdeeds takes a certain level of humility. It can often feel unnatural to be corrected for our blind spots, faults, and failures, but if we cannot open ourselves to receiving the teachings and corrections of those with wisdom and clear spiritual vision, we may not realize that we are falling into wickedness. And the fate of the wicked? Not so great. The prosperity of the wicked? Not so long.

On the other side of the spectrum, we can be a safe, trusted person for others to come to for spiritual direction and correction. Such a role requires courage, patience, trust, and love to care for the one we see hurting. Such a relationship should be mutually agreed upon by all parties.

Within the body of Christ, loving, trusted correction is necessary because it is literally a matter of life and death. The fate of those seeking the face of God is eternal prosperity; the fate of those seeking wickedness is death.

We need good mentors around us, we need to be good mentors, and we need God to speak into our lives so that we can flee temptation and stay away from what causes us harm.

Questions for Reflection

1. What qualities or characteristics make someone a good spiritual advisor/mentor?

2. Are you willing to receive correction from a few close, trusted people in your life? Do you think those trusted people know that you are open to this level of accountability?

Day Forty: Psalm 142

What Does This Mean?

Desperate times call for desperate measures. In today's poem, the Psalmist finds himself seeking divine intervention to be rescued from prison. He has come to this situation at the hands of strong enemies who have trapped him through false accusations. Overwhelmed, he pours out his troubles before God. Only God can direct him through his circumstances because only God knows his innocence.

Because of the power of his enemies, or perhaps because of just enough truth in a particular accusation, the Psalmist finds himself alone in the world. No one will help him or encourage him—he is ignored and lonely.

The author calls to the LORD in his low estate for rescue against those who are stronger than him. The Psalmist makes a vow—if God would bring him out of prison, he will thank God by giving testimony of His kindness.

What Does This Imply?

We can imagine the level of despair our Psalmist endures when we read that he faces powerful enemies who have thrown him into prison, his friends offer no help or support, and he is lonely.

To be a prisoner at this time was far from pleasant. A prisoner was isolated, sometimes starved, and existed in a cramped and dark space with little fresh air. To encounter such a place as an innocent person with no advocate or encourager explains why our Psalmist was so low.

In pain and desperation, our Psalmist turns to God for help beyond his own resources. As a kind of exchange for release from prison, he vows to speak about God's kindness. Despite his location, sense of abandonment, and loneliness, the Psalmist calls on God because he trusts that He knows of his innocence, and God surely rescues the innocent. We might imagine the Psalmist considering, if I am innocent, it means God is on my side. God is not indifferent to his situation and suffering.

How are We Invited to Respond?

There are many forms of prison. Beyond a physical building, prison can be an emotional, mental, and/or spiritual space. When we are imprisoned in an area of our lives, we may find ourselves overwhelmed by the desperation of our situation. Our circumstances may begin to feel so desperate that those around us can't (or won't) support us to the degree that we long for.

It may be that only when our enemies are more powerful than us, when we reach such a significant level of desperation and dependence, will we remember to look up. We look beyond ourselves, crying out to God for rescue from prison. We bargain, if You would do this, God, we will (insert negotiation here).

And by the grace of God, some of us will be released from our prisons with greater immediacy. Such release will invoke testimony and praise for God's kindness.

Some of us will not be quickly released from our prison. But because Jesus stood alone through judgement, alone on the cross, our prisons, though not lifted, may be transformed. Faith beams brilliant and justified on the day we enter the LORD's presence, vindicated from our suffering, having learned to say, "It is well with my soul." Christ has not abandoned us; He has aided in carrying what we thought would destroy us. A faithful Christian response to hardship involves learning to carry the lament until is transformed into something glorious.

Questions for Reflection

1. Based on what we know of this Psalm, how are we invited to carry our desperate circumstances?

2. What enables a person to say that it is well with their soul regardless of the circumstances around them?

Conclusion

A Final Word on Lament

This resource serves as a practical guide to processing through a range of experiences, griefs, sufferings, and losses.

If you've gotten to the end of this book and thought, "Now what?" continue digging through the hard things. Continue to reference this book as a resource when new storms come. Don't distract; don't numb.

If you're experiencing healing, praise God! But if you're not, God's not finished with the work of healing in your life until you are united with Him forever. God is faithful, and we demonstrate faithfulness to Him by remembering who He is and trusting that He will make a way for redemption.

"May the God of hope fill you with all joy and peace as you trust in him, so that you may overflow with hope by the power of the Holy Spirit." – Romans 15:13 (NIV)

In Christ,

Rev. Allyce Fogle-Logue

Notes

1 Tennent, Julie. "Lament." Asbury Theological Seminary Lenten Service, 2020, Asbury Theological Seminary, Wilmore, Kentucky, Sermon.

2 Tennent, Julie. "Lament." Asbury Theological Seminary Lenten Service, 2020, Asbury Theological Seminary, Wilmore, Kentucky, Sermon.

3 Augustine of Hippo. *Confessions*, Book VII.

4 Foster, Richard J. *Celebration of Disciplines: The Path to Spiritual Growth*, (HarperOne, 1998), 144.

5 Foster, Richard J. *Celebration of Disciplines: The Path to Spiritual Growth*, (HarperOne, 1998), 151.

6 Wesley, John. *Wesley's 22 Questions of Self-Examination*, 1729.

7 Interpreter's Bible Commentary: Volume IV, *Psalm 27* (New York: Abingdon Press: 1955), 144–145.

8 Interpreter's Bible Commentary: Volume IV, *Psalm 43* (New York: Abingdon Press: 1955), 225–227.

9 Interpreter's Bible Commentary: Volume IV, *Psalm 57* (New York: Abingdon Press: 1955), 296–301.

10 Interpreter's Bible Commentary: Volume IV, *Psalm 70* (New York: Abingdon Press: 1955), 369–372.

11 Interpreter's Bible Commentary: Volume IV, *Psalm 70* (New York: Abingdon Press: 1955), 369–372.

12 Interpreter's Bible Commentary: Volume IV, *Psalm 86* (New York: Abingdon Press: 1955), 462–467.

SCAN HERE to learn more about
Invite Ministries—created to invite people to a deeper
faith and living relationship with Jesus Christ